SUN BUDDHAS
MOON BUDDHAS

SUN
MOON

ELSIE P. MITCHELL

BUDDHAS BUDDHAS

A ZEN QUEST

Foreword by DOM AELRED GRAHAM

New York · WEATHERHILL · *Tokyo*

For
my parents
my husband
and
Nancy Wilson Ross
with gratitude
and gassho

First Edition, 1973

Published by John Weatherhill, Inc., 149 Madison Avenue, New York, N.Y. 10016, with editorial offices at 7–6–13 Roppongi, Minato-ku, Tokyo 106, Japan. Protected by copyright under terms of the International Copyright Union; all rights reserved. Printed and first published in Japan.

Library of Congress Cataloging in Publication Data: Mitchell, Elsie P   1926– / Sun Buddhas, moon Buddhas: a Zen quest. / 1. Mitchell, Elsie P   1926– / 2. Religious life (Zen Buddhism) / I. Title. / BQ972.I87A37 1973 / 294.3'927 / 73–4037 / ISBN 0–8348–0083–7

CONTENTS

Foreword, *by* Dom Aelred Graham   7

Prologue   *11*

1. The Temple of Infinite Peacefulness   *13*

2. The Teacher and the Precepts   *31*

3. Some Ancestors and Early Memories   *43*

4. "Perhaps You Should Get Married and Travel"   *57*

5. "Mother of God, Virgin, Be Joyful"   *65*

6. Asian Christians, Asian Buddhists   *79*

7. The Man with the Bamboo Trunk   *91*

8. The Orphan   *121*

9. In the Blue Dragon's Cave   *127*

10. A Zen Catholic Roshi   *141*

11. Some Queries   *155*

12. Lex Orandi, Lex Credendi   *165*

13. Separate Vessels   *179*

14. The Death Mask   *197*

15. Preparations for a Journey   *201*

Postscript   *213*

Acknowledgments   *215*

FOREWORD

IT MUST BE RARELY that a publisher invites a character in a story to step out from its pages, so to speak, and introduce it to its readers. Nevertheless the procedure in the present case may have a certain fittingness. I have watched this book slowly taking shape with a friendly, though not entirely uncritical, eye. In my view, it is a literary exhibition of Zen in its most vital form; but it is much more than that. It is the narrative of a young woman reacting to the religious influences of her childhood, reflecting and experimenting, living all the while in the everyday world, until, though a Westerner born and bred, she came to rest in the simplest, yet most highly evolved, religion of the East.

The story is told with an artlessness that is its own commendation. There are no literary flourishes, no purple passages, not a touch of sophistication. The Christian reader may be startled, even at times somewhat put off, by the author's negative reactions to aspects of Christianity as it is often presented. Or rather, as it was taught in her New England childhood, with the Old Testament exclusivism and intolerance sharply emphasized. Yet it is well to remember, even in these ecumenical days, that this emphasis, in parts of the Christian world, still remains, at least in an adulterated form. And in any case, there can be some benefit in Christians of today being given the opportunity to see ourselves as others see us.

On the other hand, despite occasional appearances to the contrary, there are many parallels between the author's discoveries and the message of Catholicism at its deepest. The book's theme, in its own terms, is the bringing to light or realization of what is here called the "Buddha nature" common to all humanity. The Western counterparts of this are the "Know thyself" pronounced by the Delphic oracle, the Socratic maxim that "the unexamined life is not worth living," and the culminating point made by St. Augustine in his *Soliloquies:* "Let me know myself, O my God, let me know Thee."

What lends to the book a distinctive charm are the brief verses, pregnant with suggestion, which are used as chapter headings. To the attentive reader they set the tone for the narrative that follows. The story displays a pleasing variety of personalities and places, linked together by the author's gift for detailed description, humor, and compassionate insight. A reader who might just possibly lose his way amid so much variety has only to turn to the Postscript, where everything is brought together and unified in what can only be called a brilliant yet truly moving synthesis. The author unconsciously reveals herself as an outstandingly honest and courageous spirit, telling her own story without a trace of egoism. She exhibits that characteristic of the Zen devotee she most of all admires— the art of being able "to teach without teaching." What she has to say should command the attention of a great many who will gladly learn.

AELRED GRAHAM

SUN BUDDHAS
MOON BUDDHAS

PROLOGUE

Each and every
living thing, without exception,
has the Buddha nature.
        Bussho, *Dogen Zenji*

A SCRIPTURE CHANTED in Zen monasteries, the *Butsu Myoho*, is said to contain the names of some 11,099 Buddhas and Bodhisattvas. Among these are Buddha with the Moon-face and Buddha with the Sun-face. Whether we be Sun-faced, Moon-faced, white-, black-, or tan-faced, we all have the innate capacity for enlightenment. All beings, consciously or otherwise, are ever in search of their own true nature, their Buddha nature.

A Buddha is a being who has awakened to his own true self. He has experienced what the great thirteenth-century Buddhist philosopher and Zen master Dogen Zenji* calls "being at home in a homeless home." Sun-faced Buddhas have lived long in the light of this truth, Moon-faced Buddhas only briefly.

Our own karma provides each one of us with the special

*Zenji is an honorific title meaning "Zen teacher."

11

possibilities and limitations of a distinctive era, culture, place, and family. "The Buddha nature," wrote Dogen, "is always present and effective in each moment of life and death." Our possibilities may be limitations and our limitations possibilities, in our efforts to find a place where we know with the English Catholic mystic Juliana of Norwich: "All shall be well, and all shall be well, and—all manner of things shall be well."

1 THE TEMPLE OF INFINITE PEACEFULNESS

> *There was a shower of*
> *falling leaves;*
> *the great temple.*
>
> *Shiei**

SOMETIME DURING THE COURSE of the eighth century Gautama Sakyamuni the Buddha, circumspectly disguised as a Christian saint, found his way into the stream of European consciousness. The story of Barlaam the hermit and Josaphat, prince of India, was first told in Arabic, Hebrew, and Greek. Later it was translated into French, Spanish, Italian, Provençal, and the languages of the Scandinavian countries. The Indian prince and his hermit teacher were enrolled in the Roman martyrology and accorded November 27 as their commemoration day.†

*This and all other chapter-opening verses are translated from the Japanese by Reginald H. Blyth. They are taken from his works *Haiku, A History of Haiku,* and *Zen and Zen Classics.*

†The interesting evolution of the Buddha (Bodhisattva, Bodhisat) into Saint Josaphat is described in *The Wisdom of Balahvar* by David Marshall Lang (London, George Allen & Unwin, 1957).

13

My first acquaintance with the life of Sakyamuni Buddha was not with this metamorphosed personality. I grew up among Unitarians, in a New England community that tended to regard the saints of Christian orthodoxy as zealous masochists whose exploits served principally to encourage superstition and idolatry. The Buddha was introduced to my Anglo-Protestant world not as an otherworldly ascetic in search of a wondrous afterlife, an eternal kingdom far above this profitless and impermanent world. Rather, he was presented as a "noble hero and reformer," who urged the renunciation of false gods, idolatrous ritual, and irrational, unproductive religiosity.

> "This is peace—
> To conquer love of self and lust of life,
> To tear deep-rooted passion from the breast,
> To still the inward strife;
>
> For love, to clasp eternal beauty close;
> For glory, to be lord of self; for pleasure,
> To live beyond the gods; for countless wealth,
> To lay up lasting treasure
>
> Of perfect service rendered, duties done
> In charity, soft speech, and stainless days:
> These riches shall not fade away in life,
> Nor any death dispraise."

The author of these verses, Sir Edwin Arnold, published his remarkable epic poem on the life of the Buddha in 1879. *The Light of Asia* was enthusiastically reviewed by Justice Oliver Wendell Holmes, and eighty editions of the book were sold in the United States alone. Emerson, Thoreau, and their blue-stocking friends in Concord, Massachusetts, were charmed and inspired by the goodness and selflessness of a self-reliant Buddha, who spoke to them in the language and in the values of their own times.

The version of Buddhism that absorbed my youthful attentions may perhaps be described as a kind of scriptolatry. I read detailed histories of Buddhist schools of thought and metaphysics, as well as all the translations of scriptures I could find. My mind became tightly stuffed with philosophic formulae, dates, and historic happenings, and with descriptions of remote places and appropriately exotic personalities.

After many years thus absorbed, in the late 1950s, while employed as an English tutor by Harvard University's Yenching Institute, it was my good fortune to have made many Asian friends of both Buddhist and Christian persuasions. My husband, Jack, and I began to think of spending a month or two in Japan in order to stay in a Japanese temple or temples. One day a Japanese friend, a convert to Roman Catholicism, was looking through a pile of books with peeling leather covers that I had borrowed from Boston's Athenaeum library.

"Buddha and Buddhism," he observed, "and more about Buddha. Are these books by antiquarians? Can they give you any information that does not belong in a museum? When will you come to see us in our Buddhist country? You should come and look around for yourself. You can observe how the religion of the books is different from what is in the mentality and the hearts of the people as they live their ordinary lives of every day. I think you will find some good things and some bad ones, too."

"Are you making some interesting discoveries about your Catholicism in this country?" I inquired.

"Catholicism is the same everywhere, one Latin Mass, one language, one rite (except for some so-called Eastern variation), one belief!"

"But surely there are significant differences of mentality and custom between Asian and Western Catholics?"

"Yes, of course there are differences. In fact, I have found many since I have been in your country. Some are maybe rather difficult to understand. But in the center of everything is the Mass and it is the same in every country, in the same Latin language. The Mass brings all the differences together in a great eternal harmony. I wonder if you can find such a thing as our Latin Mass within Buddhism. I do not think you can. But you must come and find out for yourself."

"It is true," I said, "that people who live here in the eastern part of this Western country usually do have a library or a museum version of Buddhism. But as long as Buddhism has been known in the West, there have been exceptions." And I read to him an excerpt from the correspondence of Emerson and Carlyle. In 1844 Emerson wrote to Carlyle: "You sometimes charge me with I know not what sky-blue, sky-void idealism. As far as it is a partiality, I fear I may be more deeply infected than you think me. I have very joyful dreams which I cannot bring to paper, much less to any approach to practice, and I blame myself not at all for my reveries, but that they have not yet got possession of my house and barn. . . . I . . . worship Eternal Buddh in the retirements and intermissions of Brahma."*

"The 'Buddh,' as Emerson called him, Sakyamuni, the founder of the Buddhist tradition, is certainly important," I said, "but it is the Eternal Buddha who resides, usually unrecognized, in all human hearts whom I would like to find during my travels and in the Buddhist temples of Asia."

Jack and I discussed with a professor of Greek philosophy from Tokyo University the possibility of visiting Japanese Buddhist temples.

"I have a friend," said the professor. "He was a student of Sanskrit at Tokyo University. Like me he was born and brought up in a Zen family temple. He is now in training for three years

*Quoted in Arthur Christy, *The Orient in American Transcendentalism* (New York, Columbia University Press, 1932).

at the historic *honzan*,* a special training temple called Eihei-ji, in the mountains of Fukui Prefecture in northwestern Japan. If you will go to Eihei-ji, I will write an introduction to my friend, Tetsuya Inoue. He will be very pleased, I think, to meet Westerners who want to understand our Japanese Zen practice."

"Elsie is interested in Buddhist chanting," my husband put in.

"Then she must hear the chanting of the many monks, as well as the voice of the great bell of the honzan. These are rather fine, I think."

"Recently," I said, "I read a description of Buddhist chanting. It is supposed to resemble the chant of the Greek Orthodox monks. Jack and I would like to take a tape recorder with us to Japan. We know of an Englishwoman who made some recordings of an Easter Week service in a Greek monastery. They are extraordinarily beautiful and so very different from most of the frightful so-called religious music one hears in this country. In fact, the BBC plans to play about twenty-four hours of her recordings next Easter. But the lady told us that the monks weren't pleased with her company, even though she is rather elderly. She spent most of Easter Week hiding with her microphone in a big basket up under the eaves of the chapel. She said that monks are afraid of women. Are Japanese Buddhist monks afraid of women?"

The professor was enchanted by the idea of the spirited Englishwoman, aloft in her basket for a week.

"That is real self-sacrifice! Self-sacrifice for beauty is one criterion of a truly civilized man or woman. I should like to meet the wonderful lady of the basket; surely she has a beautiful spirit!" said the professor approvingly. He continued: "Elsie-san will not need to hide in a basket from the monks of Eihei-ji. They will surely welcome her. If you can find a tape recorder that will go on batteries they will certainly cooperate in the making of recordings, if a request for permission to record is made in advance.

*Head temple or training temple.

And to bring such a recording to the United States is a good thing,
I think."

"Perhaps," I said, "some Westerners who hear the chanting
may want to chant the timeless sutras themselves one day."

In the autumn of 1957, Jack and I finally visited Eihei-ji, a seven-
hundred-year-old Buddhist temple located in Fukui Prefecture
about six hours' train ride from the old Japanese capital of Kyoto.
As he had promised, the professor of Greek philosophy provided
us with an introduction to his friend, Tetsuya Inoue, then in
training there. We also had an introduction to a young temple
master, Dainin Katagiri, in Kyoto, and he accompanied us on the
long slow train ride to Fukui City. From Fukui City we proceeded
by taxi over potholed dirt roads to the then-remote mountain
temple.

Eihei-ji, one of the two main temples where priests are trained
for the Soto branch of the Zen sect of Buddhism, was founded in
1244 by Dogen Zenji, one of the outstanding personalities of
Japanese Buddhism. The temple is situated on the side of a mountain and is surrounded by stately cryptomeria, botanic relatives
of the California redwoods. In winter the temple is engulfed by
six or seven feet of snow; the sun is rarely seen for a whole day at
any time of year because of the heavy fogs and rain that drift up
from the Japan Sea. The rocks and trunks of the cryptomeria are
covered with heavy dark moss and the temple compound is blan-
keted with this luxuriant vegetation, which the monks tend carefully by pulling out small weeds and grass. From April to early
December the sound of rushing water can be heard everywhere;
mountain streams flow through the temple compound and
break and fall just below the main entrance. On early autumn
mornings, just before dawn, the songs of the cuckoo and cicada

merge into the waves of chanting and deep soft sounds of the *mokugyo** that pour down the mountainside from the main shrine.

Eihei-ji comprises fourteen large buildings, as well as guest quarters and numerous smaller buildings. These are joined by long covered passages. The floors of these passages are so highly polished that one must take great care not to slip or fall as one pads up and down the endless stairs in floppy slippers. Monks and guests all leave their shoes in a special building near the main entrance.

Inside the main gate are two tall plaques on which are characters that may be translated: "Only those concerned with the problem of life and death should enter here. Those not completely concerned with this problem have no reason to pass this gate." This was translated for us by our guide-interpreter, who impressed us with his simplicity and his irrepressible cheerfulness, though he was obviously not in good health. With his help we recorded, in a number of different buildings, fourteen hours of chanting and, in its outdoor housing, the great meditation bell.

Mr. Katagiri, who had spent three years in training in the temple, was an invaluable assistant. He always knew the shortest way from one building to another, how to cool down a boiling Japanese bath for sensitive-skinned Westerners, and where to purchase fruit to augment the temple diet. One evening he nimbly climbed out of a window onto the steep tile roof to locate our microphone strategically. From the microphone trailed a heavy cord about fifty feet in length, with which Mr. Katagiri deftly avoided entanglements. "When I was in training here, I used to air the *futon,* the sleeping mattresses, out there, and I got quite accustomed to walking about over the tiles," he told us.

Most of the monks' day is spent doing manual work. The monks clean the temple, bring wood to the kitchen, make char-

*A large polished wooden drum that is struck with a heavy padded stick to establish the rhythm of the chanting.

coal, and wait on the guests. Several times a year they have *sesshin,* or periods in which to "collect the mind" in zazen meditation. During sesshin, or retreat time, nearly all the monks spend the whole day in the meditation hall doing zazen from two or three in the morning till nine o'clock at night. During the retreat periods the food is both good and plentiful. Ordinarily the monks live on watery rice and a few equally watery vegetables.

One of a novice's first tasks may be to wash the lavatory floor. After a *gassho,* palms joined in the attitude of prayer, before a small shrine near the entrance, he ties up his long sleeves, dons clumsy wooden clogs, and then washes up as quickly and efficiently as possible under the watchful eye of a senior monk. This task, preceded by the gesture of gassho, is a more significant part of a monk's life than any of the colorful and impressive ceremonies performed in the temple. In gassho, the left hand symbolizes the heart (the Buddha nature) of the greeter or the one who is venerating; the right hand, the greeted or the venerated. Monks greet each other and guests, and venerate the Buddhist images, in this way. At Eihei-ji the gassho also expresses "please," "thank you," and "excuse me." It is used by the monks before many of the most menial of their tasks, in the spirit of the Chinese Zen poet P'ang-yun: "Miraculous power and marvelous activity, drawing water and hewing wood!" The gassho is an attitude toward life. When this gesture is made quite spontaneously and automatically before a hot bath or a cup of tea, before going to the toilet, or in time of pain or sorrow, then the way of the Buddha has taken its first step beyond philosophy.

The Eihei-ji Zen master is usually available and ready to answer the monks' questions. However, the answers that the master gives are a source not of comfort but of frustration. A typical response is a pleasant smile and the reply, "Be grateful." Ordinarily, gratitude means appreciation for benefits received. However, the Zen master's "grateful" is not gratitude for any special thing or things. It is based not on discrimination but on awareness, and the temple regime and rituals help to stimulate this awareness.

For Buddhists, the most important aspect of their ritual is chanting, and chanting requires deep and disciplined breathing. A Polish Benedictine monk, Dom Cyril von K. Krasinski, has written in his interesting little volume *Die Geistige Erde* (The Spiritual Earth):* "In the Tibetan tradition of medicine, great importance is attributed to the control of the vehicle of spiritual sound! Music is considered a vital source of spiritual transformation, and vibrations are recognized as cosmic manifestations of a spiritual principle. The lamas, skilled in medicine, have developed a science as well as an art of sound. They carefully cultivate sensitivity to musical pitch and tone and to the moods thereby created, which they believe have the power to heal, or, if misused, to sicken, according to the vibrations involved. The bells and giant conch shells used in Buddhist rituals are credited with particular powers of spiritual healing."

Buddhist monotonal chant is a simple and vital form of musical expression. It is not discursive; it does not appeal to the mind or emotions, and it does not draw them into interesting involvements. An overstimulated mind and an ego with enervating defenses produce anxiety, insecurity, and restlessness in modern man, which make it difficult for him really to listen to the wind, the ocean, or music that does not express itself in a great variety of alternately exciting and pacifying rhythms and tonal changes.

Another function of Buddhist ritual is that it provides a contact with the layman. At Eihei-ji the monks' only contact with lay people is with those who come to the temple for a night, for a meal, or for one of the special observances, such as the memorial week in honor of the founder or a Precepts-taking ceremony, *Jukai*, for laymen, which are both held once a year. The guest quarters at Eihei-ji are very large; they are modern, clean, and comfortable.

*Published by Origo Verlag, Zurich, 1960. See also Hans Kayser, *Akróasis: The Theory of World Harmonics* (Boston, Plowshare Publishers, 1971).

The guests live in traditional-style Japanese rooms with cushions to sit on, a pottery *hibachi,* or charcoal brazier, on which is an iron teapot for boiling water, and a tea set. In one corner is a special raised platform on which is usually placed a porcelain bowl and above which hangs a traditional picture-scroll. In some of the rooms the paper doors are decorated with ink sketches of bamboo, birds, or fish. The guests are waited on by the monks; meals are served in each room, and the sleeping quilts are brought out every night and put away every morning by a monk attendant. These attentions, as well as the various ceremonies conducted in the temple, are one form of Buddhist gratitude. The monk is expected to share his life with all who come to the temple. Lay people, particularly if they know how to chant sutras, are enabled to share the benefits of the monks' meditation, which has been carried on through seven hundred years of uninterrupted dedication.

The visitor may spend his time taking walks in the lovely countryside around the temple or drinking tea with the senior monks when they are free. The food served to the guests is completely vegetarian. Eihei-ji's cook is a master of his art, and even when the number of visitors is large, the food is varied and good. It is served on lacquered trays in many little lacquer dishes and includes such specialties as lotus buds in syrup and tiny oak leaves fried in oil. Temple life is very agreeable for a Westerner if he can sit comfortably on his heels for long periods, doesn't mind shaving in cold water, and likes rice, pickles, and cold spinach with soy sauce for breakfast. Each meal is preceded by a chanted grace, which the monk who serves chants for those who do not know it. The day ends with a Japanese-style bath, which is one of the real delights of Japanese life. Just outside the bathroom is an anteroom where one leaves one's clothes, makes gassho, and lights a stick of incense. The incense is placed in a brass dish before a little plaque on which are characters that mean "sweet-smelling water."

One night, after the bathing hour, I passed a room where the paper door was just slightly open. Inside, a tiny little old woman with a shaven head and wearing a very worn black cotton robe was sitting on her heels in front of her hibachi. She was sitting completely motionless. It was impossible to tell whether she was asleep or awake. Her work-swollen hands were joined in gassho, and on her thin wrinkled face was the "archaic smile," the enigmatic smile of the dancing Shiva, the stone Buddhas of T'ang China, a Gothic Madonna. In that serene smile of the little old nun lay the wisdom of "being at home in a homeless home," the wisdom that cannot be taught but must be realized and lived.

The way of Eihei-ji, its Mahayana faith, ideals, and outlook, can be effectively shared with outsiders in the special quality of the traditional chant and in the great strength of the zazen silence pervading the temple in the hours before dawn. Jack and I were persuaded that sensitive, open-hearted Westerners would feel drawn to these expressions of the numinous. We left Japan with a suitcase full of recorded tapes. A good friend, Stephen Fassett, edited our recordings for an album* later brought out by Moses Asch, a venerable patron of ethnic music and founder of Folkway Records. One day, after months of working on the tapes with saintly patience and consummate artistic skill, Steve remarked: "That wonderful drum, those vibrant bells, and the extraordinarily moving chant convey an atmosphere of Shangri-La, evoke a vision of the back of nowhere. Moreover, the silences in these recordings are really just as impressive as the voices and the remarkable musical instruments! One can't help wondering if beings of a saintly or possibly even a celestial nature live in that temple of Buddha."

The first morning that we followed the long, roofed temple corridors to attend the 3:30 A.M. services, the almost unearthly quiet, a silence broken only by the rush of falling water, was indeed an experience of transcendent otherworldliness. At that time, in the late 1950s, Eihei-ji was still remote and somewhat inaccessible;

*Zen-Buddhist Ceremony, Folkways FR8980.

the tourists who stayed in the guest quarters were mostly traditional country people with courteous and dignified manners. However, even before Japan was comprised as it now is of a largely transistorized populace, and before wide, tarred roads pushed their ugly black heads right to the temple gates, Eihei-ji was inhabited by all-too-human individuals who, as one old Zen teacher put it, "sometimes went along with the Buddha but at other times went the way of *jigoku,* hell."

The life of a novice is for young men only. Zen became a sect in Japan in the Kamakura period (1185–1336), and the samurai warriors were among the first to be attracted by its vigorous down-to-earth philosophy. Present-day honzan training is a militant sort of discipline for a professional priesthood. It is exhausting for all except the most rugged country boys, some of whom, we observed, seemed to have enough superfluous energy to practice their judo holds on each other between clean-up tasks and when they thought no guest or monk was about. For the less robust sons of middle-class temple masters, or for middle-class laymen in search of answers to their spiritual questions and problems, the temple life and diet are an ordeal just short of martyrdom. Of the young Americans who have gone there for periods of training in recent years, most have left exhausted, sick, or, in some cases, greatly disillusioned. Asceticism, lack of privacy or choice, and long hours of heavy rough work in what even most Japanese consider a feudally run institution, do not of themselves produce the *satori,* or enlightenment, that people read about in books. Enlightenment is not a commodity that can be manufactured by any special regime of meditation training or austerities.

Nevertheless, my first Eihei-ji sojourn impressed me deeply. Here the atmosphere, the customs, were neither strange nor exotic, nor even foreign to me. All was familiar in a curious sort of way, and I found myself at home, an experience that was really neither reasonable nor comprehensible. The great sonorous bell, the voice of Emerson's "Eternal Buddh," spoke to all sentient hearts, and its message awakened answering voices not only from chanting monks but also from trees and flowers and the cascades of water flowing down the mountainside. Clearly, at the center of all creation there was a Great Enlightening Heart capable of endless rebirths and transformations: a Heart, or Mind, as Buddhists usually like to call it, from which neither I nor any other creature could ever become separated. This discovery was as wonderful as it was unexpected. As I sat on the tatami floor drinking ordinary hot water from an earthenware cup in the dark chill of the predawn hours, suddenly and briefly I saw through all my doubts about the nature of life. Quite inexplicably, I realized that despite the omnipresence of suffering, of destructive, competitive hatreds, of hypocrisy and endless deluding manias, there was at the heart of the matter a Great Simplicity. This familiar yet ungraspable Simplicity the Japanese have always expressed most appropriately in the music of the *koto* or flute, and in haiku:

> "The wind roars
> on the anniversary of the Buddha's death:
> the taste of the plain hot water."*

After drinking the plain hot water at Eihei-ji, I lost all taste for the cigarettes and alcoholic concoctions in which I had sometimes overindulged. It was not a question of principle. Smoking and alcohol were simply no longer a part of my life.

One afternoon during that first visit to Eihei-ji, two of the monks invited Jack and me to accompany them on a walk up one of the small, very steep hills behind the temple. It was a warm day filled with birdsong, and though it was September, the trees and underbrush were still quite green. The steep winding path was wet and slippery from the rain that had fallen the night before. The two monks were dressed in the baggy black bloomer

*Translated by R. H. Blyth in his *A History of Haiku*, vol. 2, p. 135.

suits that are their work clothes, and they slipped around a lot in the rubber *zori,* or sandals, that they wore. Nestled in the trees and bushes along the narrow path were little way stations; each contained a stone image of Kannon Bosatsu, to whom Eihei-ji is dedicated.

"Why are there so many images, and all of the same Bodhisattva?" inquired Jack. "Why is Sakyamuni Buddha not represented?"

"Kannon Bosatsu, the Bodhisattva of Compassion, is the heart of Sakyamuni, the heart of all Buddhas, the heart of the Dharma, of truth. The compassion of Kannon can be awakened in thousands of different ways in the hearts of all creatures. These images are reminders that we must not look in only one place or in one way for the Bodhisattva's compassion."

Jack and the two monks wandered off, Jack with camera in hand, in order to take some photographs of a particularly fine view of the surrounding hills. I sat alone in the warm sun, looking down at the gray slate temple roofs below. One or two elderly Japanese vacationers in rather threadbare kimono shuffled by, obviously in search of a place to eat their picnic lunch. The gentle, peaceful faces of those stone Kannons had impressed themselves on my heart, and I wondered about the nature of the compassion that they inspired. Was it more sensitive, more aware, less given to histrionics and delusive self-advertising activity than so much of our Western "charity"? Was it less abused as an aggressive expression of status and a source of popular approval than much of what passed for compassion and benevolence in my own country? "The energetics of benevolence": I often thought about that phrase of Perry Miller, the New England historian who took a long hard look at the tradition of benevolence and "service" among his fellow New Englanders. His observations resulted in a number of salutary insights into the nature of Puritan charity. Were human beings, I wondered, capable of active benevolence, of the pursuit of goodness, without giving in to the inevitable resulting frustrations and resorting to searches for scapegoats, in-quisitions, and revolutionary zealotry? Were there, or had there ever been, Buddhists who would gladly torture their fellow beings in order to achieve their own particular version of Nirvana in this world, or any other, for that matter? Evil, I could not help feeling, resulted all too often from good intentions or from single-minded utopian efforts to uplift or to reform. Every day in every way we should be getting better and better, and, if not, we must find something or someone to blame for it! Furthermore, it did not seem to me that it was always possible to know when one was engaged in activities that would result in harm or distress to others. Apologies and repentance for what has harmed or grieved, however desirable, rarely right the wrongs involved, and seemed to me more likely to bring peace of mind to the wrongdoer than compensation to the wronged.

"When we think about the limitations and ambiguities in this life of ours," the monk Tetsuya Inoue had said to me earlier that day, "I think it is really impossible to be aware of exactly where lie all the rights and wrongs. It is impossible for us always to make good choices for justice and benefit for all those around us in our families, our temples, our towns, our country. Of course we have the Precepts," and he enumerated them: "We are not to kill —this includes animals— not to steal, not to commit adultery, not to lie, not to drink, not to slander, not to insult, and not to covet. We should control anger, and finally, we must not speak falsely of the Buddha, his Teaching, or his Community. We follow these Precepts to the best of our ability, not because we think we can basically alter the nature of the world so that all will be satisfied and at peace with each other, but because we feel gratitude to the Buddha, through whom we can know the Great Mind, the Great Heart. We express this gratitude by trying to live according to the Precepts, which turn out to be very difficult and complicated so long as one is not in a state of *mushin,* complete open-mindedness and selflessness, a 'dropping off of mind and body' and living in accord with our Buddha nature. This is a state of being which is hard to know. All our lives we must do zazen to clean our minds of delusion and enable us to live in an enlightened way, in the light of the Buddha nature, which is usually so well concealed from our own and from others' view.

"To speak of what Westerners, Christians, call repentance," he continued, "we do have an important ceremony in this Zen temple where we must each make an important acknowledgment before our Dharma brothers and friends: '*Shozai muryo.*' Shozai muryo means we recognize and acknowledge that our lives are lived at the expense of other people, of other creatures, and of our home, the earth itself. I can't possibly survive unless some lives are destroyed to sustain me. Even if I do not eat the meat of fish or animals, there must still be destruction and sacrifice if my life is to be maintained. As a Buddhist, I cannot accept such sacrifice without making my best possible contribution to the welfare of these creatures, this earth of which I am a part and on which I must completely depend for my continued existence. Though I know my life will not be without mistakes, I must exert all my efforts to live in the spirit of the Eternal Buddha, to act in accord with the Buddha nature as it expresses itself through my personality and social circumstances."

I thought about this unpretentious, unvarnished, and straightforward explanation, about the voice of the Buddha, of Kannon, in the great bell and in the chanted Dharani* of the Great Heart, *Dai Hi Shin Dharani*, as I sat on the top of that steep tree-covered hill in Japan, overlooking the roof of the seven-hundred-year-old temple. The ordinary everydayness of this truth was overwhelming in its persuasive simplicity. There was also the mysterious working

---

*A *dharani*, like a mantra, is chanted not to express a sentiment or concept but in order to penetrate as deeply as possible into the spirit of the dharani or mantra in question and to realize our oneness with this spirit. Translated literally, "dharani" means "that by which something is sustained." One who recites or chants a dharani is sustained by the vibrations peculiar to it.

out of the karma, providence, which had deposited me in this place where so many questions were unexpectedly answered with so few words; and where I knew I belonged, where I was meant to be, impelled by the eternal Dharma.

The monks had spoken to us of the annual training period that they called Jukai, a week-long preparation for the taking of the Precepts. I knew that it would be the natural and obvious thing for me to take part in such a Jukai, or Precepts-taking procedure, despite the expense of another long journey to Japan, the physical discomfort, and other assorted inconveniences and difficulties. Somehow it would be possible to express my gratitude to the compassionate voice of Kannon, to the Buddha Sakyamuni and the Patriarchs, and participate in that tradition of truth-teaching that stretched back into antiquity further than my imagination could follow.

2 THE TEACHER AND THE PRECEPTS

Nothing whatever is hidden;
from of old, all is as
clear as daylight.

AFTER JACK AND I RETURNED to Kyoto I wrote to Tetsuya Inoue and told him that I wished to take part in the Jukai of Eihei-ji. I asked for books and instructions as to how this could best be accomplished.

"A Westerner has never before taken part in our Eihei-ji Jukai," replied the monk in a return letter. "However, we will send you instructions in translation of what you should memorize and what you should know about our tradition, about our way of understanding and practicing the Buddha's truth."

I entertained nagging doubts as to whether I would be able to live up to the Precepts. Not only were my inadequacies to be considered, but also I suffered from the childish notion that I would not have enough strength of mind to live as a Buddhist in a non-Buddhist country. I discussed these doubts with a Japanese Buddhist friend, and he told me the following story about an interesting man, a Buddhist of Japanese-British parentage.

Captain Jack Brinkley was a half-Japanese cousin of George Bernard Shaw, whom Captain Brinkley once shepherded around Japan. Captain Brinkley became a Buddhist after a stint in the British army during World War I. He liked to reply to Westerners' questions about the Buddhist Precepts by telling them about his first meeting with a famous *roshi,* or Zen master. This roshi was the abbot of one of Japan's historic temples. When Jack Brinkley visited him he was at the height of his career and probably had hundreds of disciples, from prisoners and policemen to a prime minister. The roshi had been in poor health for most of his life, having been abandoned as a baby to die in a snowdrift. The woodcutter who found him and adopted him was poor and had no money to attend to the child's physical infirmities. Finally, in middle age, the roshi's doctor recommended that he drink some rice wine each day, which advice the roshi seems to have followed during the rest of his life. Visitors to his room often were surprised to see a sakè bottle on his writing table. He never tried to hide his drinking. This lack of interest in his reputation was bound to displease some fellow monks, and a few lay people, too.

When Captain Brinkley visited the roshi, the first thing that caught his eye as he entered the roshi's room was a sakè bottle on the writing table. He knelt and bowed to the old monk. The roshi greeted him genially, then reached for the bottle on his table. He poured himself a drink in a Japanese cup and then offered the bottle and another cup to Captain Brinkley. Captain Brinkley refused politely but rather uncomfortably.

"Oh," said the roshi, "you don't ever drink, do you? Well, that is virtuous indeed. There is a Precept, I believe, that forbids Buddhists to drink, though not many people take it very seriously these days, I've noticed." And he took a swallow from the cup before him. "However, young man, when an abbot, the most important person in a temple, offers you a drink, it is impolite to refuse, you know. You cannot allow an abbot to drink by himself." And the roshi again extended the bottle.

Captain Brinkley, the most polite and courteous of men, refused a second time, despite mounting discomfort and embarrassment.

"So, you refuse to drink with a man who is your senior! Do you think that proves your superior virtue? Do you think that a layman is the one who interprets the Precepts in a temple when there is a master present? From whom have you learned your Buddhism, please tell me?"

Captain Brinkley replied politely but firmly that he felt he must persevere in his vow to keep the Precept, however impolite and inconvenient it might prove. And again he apologized courteously.

The roshi fixed him with a ferocious and piercing look, then there followed a few moments of silence. Finally the old man said in a severe and menacing voice: "I am the one who is to be respected and obeyed in this temple. If I say someone is to drink with me, they drink! I order you to accompany me in drinking a cup of wine!" Captain Brinkley refused still more firmly and this time with real, though still courteous, conviction.

The roshi put down his cup and laughed heartily. "Good, good," he said. "I'm glad to see that you actually have learned a little bit about Buddhism. Yes, you have begun to learn in the right way."

Jack and I were introduced to Captain Brinkley. He belonged to the Tendai sect of Buddhism, in which Zen meditation had been practiced before the development of Zen as a separate school. We asked him if he had ever been interested in the practice of Zen.

"Oh yes," he said. "I used to go to listen to Master Harada, a famous Zen master, when he spoke in Tokyo. He was a good man, quite an interesting man. Once," he continued, "I went to a retreat at a big Zen temple in Kamakura. It was in midsummer, it was terribly hot and the meditation hall was full of flies. The monk in charge saw me, a new man, in the hall for the first time. He thrashed me with his 'warning stick.'* After several hours, I went to sleep quite comfortably in my cross-legged position. The monk came again and thrashed me until his arms were probably tired. I didn't mind. Though it was rather painful, it was not unendurable, and it was what the monk was there to do, of course. After several hours of zazen, I dozed off again, as it was a very hot day and this seemed eminently sensible in such weather. Back came the young monk with his stick. By this time he was obviously very tired and cross. A few long hot days continued like that. On the whole it was quite an interesting experience in the concentration and focus of one's energies. But I didn't bother to go back to that meditation hall.

"Zen meditation is also practiced in other Buddhist temples that do not belong to the Zen sect and it is a good thing, but it is important that it be done in a Buddhist spirit. Different temples have different customs and in some meditation halls the warning stick is used with care and restraint. Actually it is meant only to induce wakeful attentiveness, to stimulate the circulation, and to relax tired shoulder muscles, nothing more. Unfortunately, the monks in charge of meditation halls are often neither enlightened nor mature. Compassionate wisdom and wise compassion are matters of individual karma, of individual development, and meditation disciplines affect individuals differently. Zazen can be badly abused, and if it becomes an end in itself some people may wander unnecessarily far from the way of the Enlightened Ones, the Buddhas and the Patriarchs. There is a name for that wild Zen, they call it the 'wild fox Zen'!"

"My husband and I have been reading the works of Daisetz

*This way of maintaining wakeful attention among meditants is standard practice in most Zen meditation halls. Meditants are whacked on each shoulder in turn with a staff called a *kyosaku*.

Suzuki," I said. "He writes a lot about monks pushing and shoving and whacking each other into enlightenment. In your experience does it often happen this way?"

"Well." He laughed. "Of course the Lotus Sutra speaks of skillful means. Most people cannot see the need for enlightenment at all and they may need to be bribed, cajoled, even tricked or possibly whacked into a knowledge of their true nature. There are many sorts and degrees of illumination. However, the *kensho* enlightenment that a few teachers talk so much about, really strict teachers rather disparagingly call 'bright toys and ornaments, candy and treats for the babies,' that sort of thing. Well, it can be said of most Zen temples, they are very clean and nicely kept up. Some of the other schools of Buddhism have become lax in their requirements for priests, so there is a lot of distasteful slovenliness. All that shouting and whacking and running about usually keeps young Zen monastics from becoming passive and sloppy."

Two years after my first visit to Eihei-ji, following due instruction and preparation, not to mention a rather egocentric preoccupation with my inadequacies, I returned to Japan, to that ancient Temple of Infinite Peacefulness. This time I went not as a visitor but as a participant in the temple life, in a monastic regime somewhat modified for lay people. The monks' diet was to be shared by Jukai participants, but heavy physical labor, such as carrying wood and polishing floors, was not expected of laymen. It was early spring, but snow was still on the ground and the large unheated halls were almost unendurably cold. Bone-chilling dampness permeated the straw tatami, the cushions and sleeping quilts. The Jukai schedule, while fairly comfortable for the Japanese country people who constituted the majority of adherents of Eihei-ji, I found very austere. It was difficult to rise at 3:30 in the black, cold morning and to sit on my heels in reposed but aware immobility for the better part of the day, which often did not end until ten at night.

The memorial services for dead monks, temple masters, and countless others appeared to stretch into an eternity. I sometimes got the fidgets, at least mental ones, though I usually managed to avoid overt manifestations except when I was exhausted at the end of a long day. When I asked my teacher-interpreter, Tetsuya Inoue, about the significance of the chanting for so many long-departed monks and Patriarchs, he replied, "For us they are a reminder of the significant personalities and deeds that constitute our long Buddhist history. For you they are zazen, and also a kind of *koan*, a problem to be resolved without the help of the faculty of reason." Now, more than a decade later, experience has persuaded me that certain kinds of lengthy ritual are indeed a far more effective means for removing delusion and for translating religious beliefs and ideals into action than is any mere preachment of doctrine. Initially, ritual should be an experience of the numinous. However, it should also be an act of self-dedication in which mind, heart, and body are brought to realization of their inherent unity with one another and with all other hearts, minds, and bodies, both present and unseen.

I often envied some of the elderly people, who, during these interminable ceremonies in the great tatami-matted teaching hall, occasionally curled themselves up in coats or blankets and took catnaps. Other elderly men and women gathered around a huge hibachi, where they drank tea, chatted, and laughed in soft high voices. The voices of the chanting monks, the wind in the trees, the song of birds, and the conversations of gnarled old country people flowed together in a deep and abiding harmony.

In the afternoons, there were a few short lectures in which simple and lucid explanations of the Precepts were given. Most of the people listened intently, and every so often an old man muttered, *"So desu"*—"That's so"—or an old woman exclaimed, *"Namu Amida Butsu"*—"Praise to the Buddha of Great Light." These comments, like the tea-drinking around the hibachi and the uninhibited napping, are a natural part of temple life.

Every evening, with the exception of the final one, there was zazen and a special ceremony called *Bussorai*. In this ceremony the participants prostrated themselves, chanting the names of various Buddhas, both historical and mythical or symbolic. Everyone took part in the hour-long procedure. By the end of Jukai week, participants were supposed to have prostrated themselves about three thousand times. I marveled that elderly people, many with arthritis or rheumatism, were able to get themselves up and down the required number of times. For me, physical activity provided a happy escape from the rigors and discomforts of long sitting, either cross-legged, for meditation, or on my heels, for ceremonies. When I told Tetsuya Inoue that I found the exercise of prostration quite self-annihilating, he laughed and said, "It is difficult to be an intellectual."

The most important rite that took place during Jukai week was the "repentance" ceremony. This ceremony is popularly understood as the confession of a kind of "original sin." Many Japanese country people enter Buddhism with childlike faith or as part of social convention and misunderstand Jukai as being only a preparation for an afterlife, which is probably why more old than young people participate. I saw very few young people among the participants of Jukai. In one of the final ceremonies of Jukai week, each participant stands before the monk-preceptor and repeats, *"Shozai muryo"*—"I commit wrongs beyond count," or "I am responsible for an infinite amount of pain and destruction in the world." Each individual's existence is responsible for more suffering than his awareness can possibly grasp. No creature can avoid bringing death, destruction, and pollution into the world. Such is the inescapable nature of things.

However, shozai muryo involves a paradox, for it is the source of gratitude for the costly gift of life as well as a resolve to limit, to the best of one's ability, the creation of suffering and waste on all levels, in every sphere of one's life. *Bonno mujin, seigan dan:* "Suffering is infinite, vow to end it all!" This vow is important because it can never be fulfilled, since fulfillment is indeed an impossibility. A haiku by the Japanese poet Issa:

> "Dew of this world
> the dew of this world cannot last
> and yet, and yet . . ."

The Jukai may eventually be followed by a second procedure called *Tokudo,* which involves a ritual acceptance of a pupil by a Buddhist teacher. Tetsuya Inoue, whom Jack and I both liked and respected, introduced me to his roshi, a saintly old monk who lived alone in a small meditation temple in Takatsuki, on the outskirts of Kyoto.

At that time Rindo Fujimoto Roshi was blind in one eye and very deaf. During the war he had refused black-market food, and his health had deteriorated accordingly. The first time I saw him he was still suffering from the effects of tuberculosis and was very frail. His *zendo,* or meditation hall, and adjoining rooms were old and drafty. The zendo, where one-day retreats were held twice monthly, had a dirt floor. In spite of the old man's infirmities, he walked daily by way of a hazardous main road with no sidewalk to a small shop to purchase buckwheat noodles and vegetables that the shopkeeper had set aside as no longer fresh. These he cooked for himself in his small crowded quarters, surrounded by his many books.

Most of the roshi's disciples were then rather elderly, though the youngest person I ever saw in the meditation hall was about six years old. They were traditional country people. One old gentleman corresponded with me quite regularly for a number of years. Some of his letters were long, and he told me about his garden, his wife's carbuncles, his children and grandchildren (the "grandgirls"), and, of course, about our mutual teacher. In one of his letters he wrote:

Mrs. Elsie Mitchell:

Thank you very much for your letter, Lady! Pardon me for neglecting to call on you in such a long time.

Do you know that Fujimoto Roshi has shut up the Taka-tsuki meditation hall and has removed to Eiten-ji to live with his disciple, Mr. Inoue?* I saw Fujimoto Roshi at our meditation meeting in his new home. He said to us, "I am very happy since my removal. Never hungry. I am able to eat three times a day! Tetsuya's wife is very kind to me. Never cold! In Takatsuki, there were many cars, many people and bad roads. Many dangers! But now, no more danger for me, so I have plenty of time to read, to write, to think. Now, I am always very happy; yes, happy and grateful always."

We all weep at heart—and are deeply moved. He is becoming a Buddha, our Great Faith Man. He does not think of other men's wrongs, he only returns good for evil.

Mrs. Tetsuya Inoue is a cultured woman and a gifted painter. In her spare time she is making a large picture— scenery, an old maple tree with red leaves, blue sky, and old wooden temple gates.

Young lady Mayako, her daughter, is growing up, faster than my last grandgirl. She grows more and more fat. She is becoming plump and quiet, shyly lovely.

It will grow cold. Take good care of yourself.

Goodbye, Lady—

Gassho

*Zen monks after leaving the honzan, or training temple, usually marry and have families. Tetsuya Inoue became the master of Eiten-ji, a five-hundred-year-old country temple in Hyogo Prefecture, in 1961. He married short-ly thereafter.

This is all of my English ability. Do not laugh, please!

S. N.

Seeing sazanka and camellia in my window.
Hearing the shrike and brown bulbul in the garden tree.

A year or so after this letter was written a Catholic Benedictine friend, in the course of a conversation with a German Jesuit author of a book on Zen meditation for Catholics, said of Fujimoto Roshi: "The roshi we met the other day at Eiten-ji, he was almost eighty, and nearly blind. Things had to be written for him to see, and he was deaf. He had goiter. He came in; you know how Japanese kneel down, and bowed to *me,* because I was to him, I presume, the Buddha nature, and he had respect for it. And he got up and was laughing, as cheerful as possible, and sat and listened. Then when he was asked a question (we had an expert interpreter fortunately), what he had to say poured forth with tremendous impact and real Zen spirit. So wise, so full of gentleness, kindness, and warmth, coming from that background, from that tradition. I was greatly impressed."

In 1961 Fujimoto Roshi had accepted me as his pupil, and it was decided that I would take part in a Tokudo at Eiten-ji, now Tetsuya Inoue's temple, in Yokawa, Hyogo Prefecture. Though I realized that I might have few possibilities for direct instruction from this gentle teacher of such heartwarming Buddhist wisdom and goodness, the sacramental aspect of the ceremony presented itself as a source of inspiration, encouragement, and good karma.

The ceremony took place on a fine but cool spring day. It was part of a four-day festivity called a *Shinsan-shiki,* the investiture of a new temple master. Two days earlier, Tetsuya Inoue had been created the new master of Eiten-ji, with his family as well as the temple's patrons and parishioners as witnesses. The Shinsan-shiki was preceded by a procession of country people up the long dirt road to the temple. All wore traditional Japanese dress, and the new temple master was transported in a traditional palanquin by two of his robust parishioners. This antique conveyance was followed by about sixty children in colorful kimono and several men carrying great sheaves of wheat.

The Tokudo ceremony, in which a master accepts a postulant disciple, was about an hour long. The Ten Precepts were chanted, and some water was sprinkled on my head by the roshi's disciple Tetsuya Inoue. The roshi's benevolent simplicity filled the tatami-floored hall. We all sat on our heels together, the roshi, his assistants, myself, and the temple's parishioners in their worn but carefully ironed black kimono. The birds' brightly persistent songs were not banished beyond the tall sliding doors, nor was the damp spring wind.

3 SOME ANCESTORS AND EARLY MEMORIES

Lighting one candle
with another candle
an evening of spring.
                        Buson

WHEN DID YOU FIRST become a Buddhist?" people often ask me. Or sometimes they inquire dubiously, "When were you converted?" I am not fond of that word "conversion." It suggests a convenient shift of behavioral gears in order to embrace a more rewarding way of life. This is often a very desirable event when there is no accompanying fanfare of chestbeating, preoccupation with guilt, and subsequent searching out of scapegoats. However, the convert mentality all too often involves a conviction of newly achieved superiority of one sort or another. Conversion is supposed to involve the sacrifice of self; but don't there remain the questions of who is sacrificing what, and for whose ultimate benefit? As for the resulting changes in personality or character, they may or may not be desirable, depending on the point of view from which they are scrutinized. They rarely escape the Zeitgeist. One generation prizes normalcy above all things; its children are drawn to becoming "all the things our parents feared."

Enveloped in a newly found euphoria of self-confidence and security of conviction, a person who has recently undergone conversion is in danger of forgetting that our fondest hopes and ideals are always interlaced with egotistical preoccupations and limitations. What we love we fear for, and what we fear we also hate. Hatred-inspired vigor in spiritual matters is eminently self-defeating and, worst of all, disposes us to become what we hate.

As regards my ever-growing preoccupation with and absorption in the tradition of Buddhism, I can only say it has made me very happy, although the Buddhist Precepts are not always either comfortable or convenient to live with. Furthermore, I am not able to judge the extent or degree of my *self-ishness* at any given period in my life. Possibly one's ego is most overstimulated when the conviction of egolessness is present.

As I look back over the years, not only of my own life, but of the lives of my immediate ancestors, my karma seems to have developed with remarkable continuity. In retrospect, I see the importance of certain events and relationships that illuminated the way—the way we are all following, knowingly or not, in search of our true selves and of our destinies.

I was born in Boston in 1926. Bostonians of English descent are often very aware of their ancestors and of their ancestral karma. Perhaps this is a result of being born, brought up, and possibly dying in a house in which things are rarely thrown away, and by being surrounded during one's early years not only by ancestral faces looking down from large gold frames but also by artifacts, furniture, clothes, books, letters, and diaries that elicit a response from that aspect of our forebears living on in us, their descendants, through succeeding generations.

A dim awareness of our Buddha nature and a desire to expand this awareness may develop in our earliest years. Scrutiny of childhood and adolescent memories may disclose important beginnings of an awakening. One of my first such memories involves my paternal grandfather. He had a splendid library that included many rare and wonderful volumes on mythology and religion, particularly the religions of ancient Egypt and India. On several occasions, either as a special treat or perhaps as a distraction, my father persuaded grandpa to show me his imposing leather-bound facsimile of *The Papyrus of Ani*. I was placed in grandpa's lap as he sat in the black leather chair in his den. On the table before us rested the big book. As the pages, too large and cumbersome for a four-year-old child to turn alone safely, were opened, an enchanted realm was disclosed. Ani, citizen of ancient Egypt, and his wife are prepared for their journey to the underworld, for encounters with a profusion of deities, animal and human, and for final judgment before the jackal-headed Anubis, who weighs the hearts of men against the feather symbol of the Law on his scales.

Ani and his wife are portrayed adoring the scarab-headed god of the morning, who is seated on his solar bark and floating on the heavens with an altar and a giant lotus flower before him, while two spirits of the dawn raise their hands in adoration. "Praisings and glorifications of coming forth and entering in the netherworld," proclaims the caption under this pleasingly bright picture, in which hues of brown and yellow predominate. The hieroglyphic text follows the couple's progress through mysterious encounters with the occupants of the nether regions. Myriad transformations culminate in a state of bliss, the final reward for Ani, the virtuous citizen of Egypt, and for his equally virtuous wife.

"Sam, the child has had enough of all that." Grandma liked to have all the children congregated together in the sitting room for charades and musical chairs. She read to us from the books of Oz, though occasionally this delight was foregone in order to remedy our lack of religious education with portions of the Bible, particularly the Old Testament. That gloomy strife-filled saga, over whose restless personalities brooded the hypersensitive and testy Jehovah, provided a bleak contrast to the tale of the beautiful land of sun and moon, inhabited by predominantly compassionate animals and humans, and to the wonders of giant lotus and serenely drifting sun bark.

"Sam's books are not for children," said grandma.

"Cousin Sam, do you think anyone ever went to the Egyptian heaven?" someone asked.

"Who knows, who knows?" said grandpa pensively from somewhere behind his wiry white whiskers.

My paternal grandmother was a Unitarian, as her mother had been before her. My great-grandmother was born in Boston in 1835 and died there thirty-six years later after the birth of her sixth child. Philosophic and religious questions preoccupied her adolescence, and at the age of fifteen she started a diary in which she recorded her doubts and observations. She read Goethe and Voltaire and was impatient with the social and domestic role that conventional ladies were supposed to play in nineteenth-century Boston. In 1853, she wrote in her journal: "How can men be so blind as to imagine that they will be happier with a wife who knows about nothing but *puddings* and *pies*. Bulwer says 'give me the woman who can echo all thoughts that are noblest in men!' *Puddings, and pies!* Bah!

"I feel a desire to learn, to find out truths, but then I become bewildered. It is certainly weak-minded in one who has resolved to search *after* truth, even if the search should tear down illusions or supports to which the mind has fondly clung for years, to fall back in terror at the very commencement. No, no, I have commenced, I have already doubted much which perhaps most women would fear to question, and now that the doubts have come, in order to dispel them, I must *think*. And what if I had never met with certain friends who have talked much to me? Would these thoughts have come to me, though perhaps later, through books, or my own observation?

"What a field of investigation is before me! But if there were nothing to study how insipid life would be. Our friend, Mr. George Brown, took tea with us today. He and I had a long discussion on faith and he endeavored to support the doctrine that sinfulness attaches to unbelief as if it were an act of volition. We talked for a long time but we differ so fundamentally that it is perhaps hardly worthwhile, yet I like to hear different ideas. Mr. Brown suggested the idea that doubts were the direct instigation of the devil—at which notion I was guilty of laughing."

A few days later she wrote: "This evening I am in rather a tumultuous yet tired state of mind. I went to church all day and then Mr. Brown called in the evening to take me to hear Dr. Twing who preached very long, so that I became excessively tired. I suspect that the aforesaid Brown feels apprehensive for my spiritual safety, he asked me if I should feel 'safe' to die in my present state of mind. I told him, yes, that I believed myself in the hands of a merciful Creator, God grant that I may at least retain that faith!

"It almost frightens me sometimes to find how I have wandered from the beaten track of opinion and yet what can I do? I must go on, *ought* at least, steadily diligently and faithfully. 'Be still sad heart.' But it isn't still, I am too young yet to expect that. I wonder if the time will ever come when my ideas will be settled and quiet. Perhaps I shall die first."

My great-grandmother's second daughter, who was grandpa's wife, was far less cerebral than her mother. Nevertheless, she and her friends read Latin and Greek plays together, a fashionable pastime in Boston in the 1880s. As a young girl, grandma preferred whist, tennis, and boating to extensive intellectual and spiritual explorations. Unitarianism was no longer a spiritual adventure at the end of the nineteenth century, and my grandmother wrote the following wry observations of the minister of the church to which her family belonged:

"We have taken a pew at Price Collier's Unitarian Church. Everyone in the family likes him excepting me. Of course he is handsome, brilliant and talented. Still, with all these qualities, I think a minister needs something different, especially in a Unitarian Church, where the minister plays so important a part. The family are all disgusted with me for not liking him, but I cannot help it. He does not seem quite genuine to me, and his words are brilliant, nothing more. . . .

"Who should call during the evening but the all-fascinating minister P. Collier. He came on horseback, booted and spurred, he also wore riding costume and looked very au fait* and offhand. He speaks with a great deal of manner just as he does in the pulpit and is apparently very affected. Every movement seems to have its object. Of course he did not speak to me, but I had a chance to scrutinize him while he talked with Grandma. This is what I saw. A man of about twenty-five, medium height, a slight, but well-made figure, very dark eyes, hair and beard, handsome teeth and beautifully shaped hands, a prononcé manner and a decided air as if he was used to being admired and liked it. So much for his personal appearance, as to what he said, his plain remarks I mean, without the accompaniment of his face and voice, they did not seem very remarkable. Beauty goes a great way and ancestry makes up the rest."

By the time my grandmother and I had become acquainted with each other, she had accepted the worldly limitations of her church and its fashionable ministers. She attended regularly and was persuaded that her small grandchildren belonged there, too. My parents were not interested in churchgoing. However, one fine spring morning grandma finally persuaded my father to have

*She meant *comme il faut,* "just so." "Au fait" was a popular Victorian expression that had become divorced from its French meaning.

me washed and brushed and delivered in my best clothes to the church door, where she and one or two of my cousins awaited me on the steps. It was "plant Sunday," father told us. Children who sat and listened attentively would be given plants as a reward for good behavior. My cousins and I followed grandma into the clean white church, down the red-carpeted aisle and into a white wooden pew with a red silk cushion. My cousin Bill carefully closed the little white door behind us. Like a lot of cows all in the same stall, I thought. The talk was interminable; the hymns were ponderous.

In the middle of what appeared to be an intimate chat with the deity, cousin Bill pulled an old stub of a pencil and a piece of dirty scrap paper out of his pocket. He was seated between me and the door of the stall. Grandma was absorbed in the sermon and did not see him write slowly in large capital letters: "QUOTH THE RAVEN NEVERMORE!"

"How clever Bill is," I thought. Underneath this pronouncement Bill drew a large, hideous face while I watched in absorbed fascination. I was still engrossed in the details of the developing face on the scrap of paper when another cousin gave me a kick and pointed to the plant carts that were, incomprehensibly, being wheeled down the aisle.

"Look what they gave us!" I cried to Maudie, my nurse, holding out my begonia for her to admire, after my return home. "Bill and I got the biggest plants on the cart because we were so close to the front of the church and Bill pulled me after him so fast. Marion was too slow and she just got a little one." Marion, another cousin, went to church nearly every Sunday; she was a good child, with a happy and docile nature.

"What did the minister talk about?" inquired Maudie stiffly. She didn't seem to notice my begonia. I thought a moment and then replied, "QUOTH THE RAVEN"—I paused for effect and concluded triumphantly—"NEVERMORE!" I tried to look as enigmatic and mysterious as my cousin Bill, and I must have succeeded. For once, Maudie had nothing more to say. She turned sharply on her heel and was off to attend to my baby brother, who was howling in his crib.

On subsequent Sundays, pressure was brought to bear for more churchgoing. Bill's company made the outing rather fun, despite the infinitely tedious talk. One Sunday, after the service was over, we sat together on the church steps. Bill had his ever-ready pencil stub and paper scraps.

"God, god, god," I said. "What does Dr. Pomeroy mean by god? And in those awful hymns, god, god, god some more."

Bill fished out a dirty scrap of blue paper from the pocket of his corduroy knickers.

"Look," he said in an authoritative sort of way, and he wrote: "God = Santa Claws." I thought about that, then Bill took back his paper and carefully wrote: "Santa Claws = God." "It can even be proven mathematically," he said sagely.

He continued: "And who do you find if you undress Santa Claus and pull off his beard? Why, your own father, of course!" I had made this disappointing discovery myself the Christmas before. I had asked a department-store Santa Claus for a special and very expensive doll, then confidently informed my mother that she and father need not bother to give me the doll in question, as Santa Claus had absolutely promised to attend to the matter himself.

"But dearie," mother protested, "Santa can't give you anything that we don't buy for you."

Consultation with school friends brought forth the revelation that Santa's presents were indeed paid for by parents and that the white-haired and -bearded being in red clothes actually was an invention of parents. "To make us good, I suppose," I had said in a disgruntled way.

"Why," I asked Bill as we sat among the milling about of adult legs on the church steps, "do people go in there every week and listen in such an interested way to Dr. Pomeroy go on about a being who is only make-believe?"

Bill shrugged: "You like to have people read you stories even though they are all about make-believe people, don't you?" I did indeed. But the church stories were gloomy and dull, and after Bill returned to his home in New York, I begged to be relieved of the churchgoing ritual.

"All right," said mother. "I don't enjoy it and don't go myself. I hated being made to go when I was your age, but mama insisted. Pa went for nice long walks in the woods, while we had to sit in church. However," mother added, "go just once to the Sunday school in the Parish House, you might like that a lot better."

Reluctantly, the following Sunday I marched off with the other children into the Parish House after the opening hymn and prayer of the adult service. I did not know anyone there, though Milton was a very small town in those days. No one spoke to me. The minister's wife was the Sunday school teacher, and she decided to tell us a story. As it filtered into my half-fixed attention, the tale came through thus: Long ago, somewhere in a distant foreign country, there was a man who was his parents' favorite child and who was given a many-colored coat, a pretty special coat, in fact. The brothers of the man with this special coat were envious. They picked on the favored one until he died and then they took away his fine coat. The ever-watchful deity called Jehovah fixed those jealous brothers for tormenting the man because of his wonderful coat; he really made them good and sorry they'd ever got at their brother and snitched his fine coat for themselves.

The minister's wife then asked us children what we thought about the man with the coat, and the brothers, and the anger of that god called Jehovah. When my turn came, the lady minister asked me to tell her why Jehovah did what he did to those jealous brothers; at least, that was what I thought she had asked me. I stood up and said I thought Jehovah surely didn't care for bullies, then added what seemed like a relevant afterthought: "Jehovah could have solved everybody's problems best by first bringing the dead man back to life." Obviously this would amount to a minor undertaking for an Almighty Being. "And," I continued, "by giving beautiful coats to each of the jealous brothers, who must have felt pretty bad being no one's favorite and because no one had given *them* fine coats and things. It's not nice at all when *you* are not the favorite," I said firmly.

Apparently this was not the right answer. The other children turned and stared, which made me squirm uncomfortably. The teacher went on and talked more about the Santa Claus–god as if he really were not just make-believe and as if he were right there listening to what she was saying about him. It was as though he sat before us with his false white hair and woolly beard, casting an eye about for people to chastise with his ferocious temper and onward-marching soldiers, about whom we had to sing; another eye he kept peeled for his favorite people, his "chosen few," whom he'd presented with some kind of presents called covenants. I had no idea what a covenant was and I didn't want to know.

Outside the Parish House window, the spring-clad trees beckoned with long green arms and birds sang their bright, free songs. That was my last day of Sunday school. My mother sympathetically agreed there were far better things to do on Sunday.

Until my eighth year I led a very sheltered life, and an uneventful one. I went to a small "progressive" school, where I had about ten equally sheltered classmates. The small beings who toddle through present-day supermarkets, surveying cellophane-swaddled offerings, know very little about where these edible substances come from. My brother and I knew still less about the source of our daily meals, and nothing of the labors that went into their preparation. In our household, children were not permitted in the kitchen. My younger brother and I rarely left our nursery playroom except to go to school or to run about the garden and woods around our house. Our lives were quite devoid of opportunities to observe for ourselves the more elemental and ferocious ways in which living creatures, human and otherwise, compete for food, shelter, and dominance over one another. Poverty and death were words that belonged in fairy stories, tales in which all was finally put right by benevolent fairy godmothers and triumphantly righteous princes.

In my eighth winter, when my mother was in poor health, the family pediatrician decided I should be sent off to the Maine countryside. The doctor, an amiable puritan in whom my parents had infinite confidence, urged that I be placed in a children's camp in the northern woods. He persuaded my parents that such an experience would result in benefits both physical and psychological.

In the 1930s the countryside on the banks of Maine's Androscoggin River was cold and remote. There was no electricity in the small cheerless wooden houses; kerosene lit the lamps and wood the kitchen stoves. The couple with whom I was sent to live were a young retired schoolteacher and her husband. The farmhouse, which they had inherited from the husband's foster mother, was a very small summer camp for a few weeks each year. In winter the couple and an aged man called Gramp devoted their time to an endless round of domestic chores, snow shoveling, and the consumption of a cellar full of glass-jarred tomatoes and string beans and stores of small potatoes, all grown in the stony fields below the house. An old station wagon with torn celluloid curtains was wound up like a clock for grocery expeditions into town when the weather was good, and in winter the six-mile journey was made in a rough seatless sleigh drawn by a bad-tempered old horse.

The farmhouse was full of books, most of them pedantic and tedious. Occasionally, book in hand, I spent the day in the barn, where lived the old horse, a Shetland pony, a pig, and some chickens. Often I sat in the pig pen and talked to Pig, a friendly being with remarkably human eyes. On cold days I crawled into the manger of the Shetland pony's stall. The pony grew a luxuriant coat, and as the barn was without heat, I eagerly sought his company despite his often bared teeth and flattened ears at my approach. Bribes of corn eventually won the woolly fellow's friendship, and his heavy breathing filled the manger with warmth and reassurance.

Early one morning a large truck drew up in front of the barn and into it the family pig was alternately pulled and kicked.

"They are hurting him," I cried to Gramp, pulling his arm. "Can't you stop them?"

"He don't know any better, it's just an animal." Gramp left off chewing his cud long enough to shake me off his arm and then to spit into the ankle-deep mud around his heavy boots.

"He's got blood on his face!" I screamed. The truck drove slowly over the hill, but Pig's cries rang in my ears the rest of the day and filled my dreams that night.

A day or so later, the master of the house returned from town with many white-paper packages. He was in high spirits.

"Pork with applesauce—real Maine bacon!" he exclaimed, opening one of the packages. Out of the white paper rolled two pig's feet. I fled to the barn and vomited into the pony's manger.

"Don't you care?" I asked my friend fiercely. "How do you know that you won't be the next? Blood all over your face, and then nothing, nothing but a lot of little pink pieces on somebody's plate!"

"Don't cry, dear." The man's wife wearily wiped my eyes with a lacy and faintly violet-scented handkerchief. "It isn't our pig, it's someone else's." The gentle, tired face was all concern. "It's just this life, everything is so expensive and everyone here is poor. It's as hard for the people as it is for poor Pig."

"Spoiled! Just a spoiled little city girl," her husband said in exasperation.

The mayflowers bloomed early under the patchy snow, and the days grew longer. One morning a large black car drew slowly up the winding dirt road. A tall white-haired lady and a little girl about my own age were helped out of the car by a uniformed driver. The child had thick golden curls that hung well below her waist, bright pink cheeks, and watchful green eyes.

"I say, do we really pee in this thing and then keep it in the room all night?" the golden-haired girl demanded as she inspected the large chamber pot in the bedroom that we were to share.

"It has a cover somewhere," I said lamely, "and in the morning we have to empty all the pots in the bathroom, all except for Gramp's, which is too heavy and has no top."

"Putrid," said Golden Girl in her brisk English voice.

The days were long, and as possibilities for amusement were limited, Golden Girl and I got into considerable mischief and were often in trouble. One very warm morning, our overseer's enduring and heroic patience cracked. "You girls are just more than I can take today. You are to sit in your room and not talk. Not one word from either of you for an hour. Not one word!"

"She's a witch," hissed Golden Girl.

"She's young and pretty. Witches are always old and ugly," I said.

"The nuns in my school in France told us that the Devil loves beautiful women. He makes them his possessions, and then they become witches without anyone finding out. Except God! He has a big eye and sees absolutely everything."

Our shrill whispers were overheard. I was banished to Gramp's bedroom, a small, smelly room on the ground floor. I sat on the window seat and stared morosely out the window. The trees were turning green, and the cows lay in the spring sun. My eye wandered about the dirty clutter of the room to the unmade brass bed with its urine-stained sheets, beside which was the unemptied chamber pot. The sun was warm. I closed my eyes, and a very different scene passed fleetingly through my mind. A month or so earlier the Androscoggin, swollen by heavy rains and melting snow, had overflowed its banks, carrying houses, barns, and animals from low-lying areas. Golden Girl and I had begged Gramp to take us with him to view the disaster from a nearby hill. There a small group of farmers and an old woman stood watching the moving water as it carried walls, furniture, chicken houses, ragged mattresses, and an occasional dead cow to a destiny somewhere beyond the horizon. No one spoke. The farmer next to us raised his hand to his head, his heart, and both shoulders, then turned and walked quietly away, the bitterness slowly fading from his eyes.

"What does that mean?" I asked Golden Girl, who always had an explanation for everything.

"It means he's a Catholic and that his God is blessing him. It's wonderful and mysterious. But it's only for Catholics. None of the mysteries work for Protestants like us even though we buy a rosary. And they don't work for animals like that poor cow all swollen up with water and being carried off to sea."

"Why not?"

"Catholics think God has just worked it all out that way," said Golden Girl. "Catholics believe they are the Chosen People. Protestants, they believe, are devils, and no one seems to think God has time for animals. He has counted the sparrows, all the sparrows in the universe. But as for animals, He allows them to have their throats cut, their hearts and eyes torn out. It's also quite all right with Him when they are cooked and eaten by greedy human beings like you and me."

4 "PERHAPS YOU SHOULD GET MARRIED AND TRAVEL"

We human beings
squirming among
the flowers that bloom.
                    Buson

WHEN I WAS SIXTEEN I went to boarding school in Farmington, Connecticut. There I read a lot of philosophy, particularly Schopenhauer and Montaigne. Montaigne's essay "Apologie pour Raimonde de Sebond" particularly impressed me. In this long, rambling tract, in the guise of a defense of Catholic orthodoxy, the philosopher passionately attacks all dogmatic certitudes. Ethics, he demonstrates with copious examples from the writers of Greece and Rome, are a matter of custom; religious creeds vary according to time and geography, and zealous creeds create bigots who devote themselves to ruinous savagery. Montaigne lived in a time, like those turbulent early forties, when Europe was awash with blood. Zealous religions, like zealous politics and chauvinism, brought delusive, destructive messianism.

I encountered another fruitful observation in one of Montaigne's essays: "Men are tormented by the ideas they form of things, not by the things themselves." This line of thought I pursued into an engrossing volume on Eastern philosophy by L. Adams Beck. In her chapter on the teaching of the Buddha she wrote: "'He who perceives with truth and wisdom knows there is no "it is not," there is no "it is."' . . . That is to say everything is at every moment passing into fresh forms of being, as a flowing river is ever and never the same. . . .

"Yet underneath all these changes and becomings and passings lies something subjective that is, that does not change. Each change is caused by some inherence in itself, some law which it is compelled to obey. It is not arbitrary. It has a steadfast sequence. And too much emphasis cannot be laid on the fact that we find the Buddha making a statement more than once on this point, which he declined to analyse or explain.

"'There is an Unborn, an Unoriginated, an Uncompounded. Were this not so there would be no escape from the world of the born, the originated, the compound.'

"In other words Reality, the Unchanging, underlies the world of appearances, of things as they are not.

"All this is law. From this law nothing is exempt, from the mightiest of astronomical systems to the microscopic life of which science has only lately become aware. And all life is one in stone, plant, insect, animal, man."*

One person who provided me with great inspiration during those school years was an elderly teacher of German. Ida Clough was a shy New England spinster who had spent much of her life in Germany studying while caring for an ailing, and undoubtedly domineering, father. Fluent in seven languages and with a doctorate in German literature from Heidelberg, her enlightened blend of literary passion and detachment was the great joy of my bookish adolescence. In her German class we read together the

*L. Adams Beck, *The Story of Oriental Philosophy* (New York, New Home Library, 1942), pp. 168–70.

lyric poetry of German writers of the eighteenth and nineteenth centuries: Schiller, Goethe, Eichendorff, Mörike, Lenau, Storm, Hebbel, Platen, and finally my favorite, Heine. The great Romantics, and particularly their preoccupation with man's relationship to nature, impressed me deeply. Sometimes I spent half the night squeezed in the back of my clothes closet, flashlight in hand, where I read with unappeasable appetite. Heine's *Buch der Lieder,* the *Winterreise,* and parts of the *Harzreise* I completed in a final orgy of youthful enthusiasm during my last semester before graduation.

The old lady nodded kindly as we shook hands on graduation day. I told her that I was feeling restless, that I was gripped by a compelling wanderlust.

"Perhaps you should get married and travel," she suggested lightly. "For those who need to spread their wings and soar, travel is just the thing. Do marry sensibly, though," she added as an afterthought.

One cold gray afternoon, many years later, accompanied by only two of her old friends, a teacher and his wife from the school, by her erstwhile pupil, and by a clergyman procured by an undertaking establishment, Miss Clough was laid to rest in her family's plot at Cambridge's Mount Auburn Cemetery. A few biblical formulae were pronounced, of the sort that are supposed to reassure traditional New England Christians that they and their world have not lived and labored in vain, and that was all. But Miss Clough was no longer a prisoner of her New England-bred "self-respect," her turn-of-the-century woollies, her myopic vision and uncertain hobble. The clergyman's platitudes fell dully into the newly turned earth; the chill wind carried away his words with the dry brown leaves.

> *"Doch frisch und fröhlich war mein Mut.*
> *In meinen Adern, welches Feuer!*
> *In meinem Herzen, welche Glut!"*

"Yet fresh and joyful was my spirit.
In my veins such fire!
In my heart such a glow!"
                (Goethe, "Willkommen und Abschied")

While still incarcerated in boarding school and isolated from
that most interesting male half of the human race, I sometimes
made excursions into the realms of what-might-be in my future,
and I developed a fairly detailed mental portrait of my future
husband. Probably he should not be an American, and thus our
lives together would not be wasted on the inanities of football,
baseball, or a variety of other tiresome folksy distractions which,
in my observation, absorbed the average American male during
his leisure hours. He would be strong and distinguished-looking,
love gardens and animals, and abhor hunting. My dream man
would not be avid for status or power over others, and he would
definitely not be a chauvinist in the matter of nationality. This
ideal mate whom I had dreamed up for myself would be at home
everywhere and would be as eager as I to cross as many new
thresholds as possible where language, customs, values, and even
race were different from his own. He would accomplish this
easily and gracefully, wishing always for expanded horizons.

I was sure that karma even then was at work on this important
person with whom I would spend many years of my life, with
whose karma my own would become enmeshed. Thus it was no
great surprise that I should meet and, shortly thereafter, marry
Jack. My husband, an Englishman born in Austria of German
and Scottish-Austrian parents, has spent only about seven years
of his life in England. He is a Roman Catholic who has not participated in any of the spiritual activities of the Roman church
since before his student days at M.I.T. His Catholicism is rather
less important to him than his British passport. Both he and his

father cherish their British passports as they do their eyes or their teeth, from which they expect a lifetime's durability.

A friend once inquired of Jack: "If you plan to live in America, why remain British?"

Jack looked mildly puzzled. "England is only one place where British people live. They live all over the world! And, after all, the States were once British colonies, weren't they?"

During the first years of our marriage, we did a lot of traveling together in Europe. We made visits to my husband's hospitable family, both in England and in Austria.

Austria is a staunchly Catholic country. People in the countryside greet each other with *"Grüss Gott."* On learning that I thought of myself as a Buddhist, Jack's Austrian cousin Stephan said to me, *"Grüss Dich Gott, Elsie, oder muss ich Buddha sagen?"*

Everywhere in the Austrian countryside are large crucifixes with lifelike and often life-sized figures of Christ, realistically harrowing. "What do you think of when you look at them?" I inquired of one of Jack's cousins.

"I am reminded that life is short and goodness is not natural for humanity," he replied. I said I thought such an image must surely stimulate sadism. It seemed to me that the history of Christendom indicated that Christians have more often crucified others than been crucified themselves.

"They have a predilection for crucifying each other, too," he reflected, "but what should not be forgotten is that all ideals are potentially dangerous and nearly all zealots are cruel."

One day cousin Stephan invited me to ride behind him on his large, bright red motorcycle. His wife and my husband were to drive to the well-known church of Heiligenblut by car, and we were to go on the shiny mechanical steed. Cousin Stephan had spent much of his life involved with powerful machinery. He had had a long career as a pilot first in the air force of Italy, then of Austria, and finally of Germany.

I had ridden behind my husband on his small American motorcycle, but Stephan's was much larger and made a great deal more noise. We set off with an ear-shattering blast. Through the lakeside tourist towns we were projected with stomach-scrambling speed. Trucks, cars, pedestrians, and chickens scattered at our approach, and I clung to the driver feeling like the appendage of an apocalypse. At first I was terrified, then exhilarated, and finally it seemed as though I had just dissolved: no more me, only the ear-rending noise and unfettered speed. Suddenly, as suddenly as the whirlwind ride had started, it stopped and I slid numbly off the rear seat onto a grassy bank. "Whatever do you have for nerves?" I inquired weakly.

"Were you frightened?" he asked.

"It is impossible to feel anything at all going like that! Is that the idea, perhaps?"

We walked through the courtyard of the ancient church. "Come," he said, "I'll show you something you may not have in America. Have you ever seen a *Knochenhaus?*" I had never seen or heard of a bonehouse. New England churches had nothing so mundane or so intimate.

On a hillock above the church and cemetery stood the bonehouse, a sort of large doghouse with an iron gate in front. Inside were stacked rows of skulls, regimented so that their hollow-eyed stares all faced us. On one side of the skulls were legs; on the other side, facing them, arms and torsos were piled neatly one on top of another.

"What a clattering and rattling there will be in there on the Day of Judgment. 'Hey you, that's my leg!' 'No, it's mine!'"

"And will you be in there one day?" I asked.

"Any day now, child, it could be any day."

"Why don't they burn the bones or grind them up or something?"

"The church doesn't permit unnatural things. Everything has to happen naturally."

"One of my great-grandmothers was burned and sprinkled in her garden over her favorite roses," I said.

Stephan looked incredulous. He obviously didn't believe me. Finally he said, "There must be cheaper fertilizers."

"No doubt," I replied. "But she thought it was the most natural and the most beautiful place to be."

"Were her ashes spread about by a priest?" he asked carefully, trying to disguise his reactions to such an alien possibility.

"Probably not."

"Well," he said thoughtfully, "I am not a very believing person, and it is all the same in the end, I suppose."

"The end is important for Catholics, isn't it?" I asked.

"Some think so. Do you?"

"It shouldn't be," I replied. "But I have often wondered about it. What do you think are the most important things in life?"

"Well, if you had asked me that ten years ago, you would have had a lot to listen to. I could tell you one thing now. To-morrow I might have something very different to say. But I do like good schnapps. Then, men and women need each other. But a little kindness, just a little kindness is what seems to me to make life bearable in the long run."

One need be neither a Buddhist nor even an admirer of the Buddha and the Patriarchs to become aware of the need for enlightenment; and this awareness is a manifestation of the Buddha nature.

5 "MOTHER OF GOD, VIRGIN, BE JOYFUL"

I know not from what temple
the wind brings the
voice of the bell.

Basho

OUR EUROPEAN TRIPS usually included visits to France. The first was in the early summer of 1947, the culmination of our honeymoon. We stayed in a very grand apartment in Paris on the rue de Lille with charming friends of my in-laws. Malcolm Béranger had lived in Thailand, then known as Siam, where he was purchasing agent for the king. If the king needed a hundred grand pianos for assorted wives and concubines, it was Béranger who found them and the means of transportation to the East. He was a collector of jade and ivory, and his collection also included many large and extraordinarily beautiful figures cut from all manner of semiprecious stones. The apartment had been decorated with these treasures as points of focus; special lighting and color schemes set off each piece and drew the eye to the color and texture of the rare carvings. A particularly arresting feature was the heavy embroidered curtains that replaced doors between some of the rooms. "The king's trousers they once were," Monsieur Béranger told us.

Paula Béranger, daughter of a Prussian general, was married to this charming if feckless gentleman of French-Scottish ancestry. Old Béranger was an enormous gray bear of a man, with myopia and the tastes of an Eastern potentate. He was never very kind to either his wife or various mistresses, but he was sweetness and generosity itself to us. His bedroom-study contained the only double bed in the apartment. He moved out of this room with its piles of leather-bound books, scattered papers, and faded photographs, and we were duly installed in his big soft bed. The first morning at breakfast we were introduced to a novel collection of guests that included a bank president from the provinces, the architect brother of old Béranger, and a homeless, impoverished French family who had only recently returned to France from years of Japanese internment in Singapore. The couple were a distinguished white-haired pair, both very frail and wrinkled. Their son, an enormous dark man probably a little older than Jack and I, was in his early twenties.

Everyone came to breakfast in pajamas—some of the guests had borrowed theirs from their host—and they wandered into the dining room from various rooms in the large apartment, where they had spent the night on mattresses spread out on the floor Japanese-style. These were produced by Kim, the Vietnamese manservant of all work, who also whisked the sleeping arrangements away in the morning. At breakfast, wrapped in their host's voluminous silk night gear, the guests sat around the large dining room table for three or four hours. Everyone introduced himself amid much bowing and kissing of hands. Meanwhile, Madame Béranger inspected the *petits pains* for mold, the one domestic task that could not be left to Kim. An enormous Pekingese called Sing Tow sat on a silk brocade chair next to his mistress and solemnly surveyed the proceedings.

We usually left long before the breakfast party had evolved into lunch, at which time Kim brought on an Oriental delicacy to be passed around well into the afternoon. The conversation was catholic, and favorite topics drifted round and round at different levels in the smoke-filled room—in French, in German, occasionally in English. War and peace, peace and war, love of this kind and that were the topics most often on everyone's lips.

"You are Buddhists," said Malcolm Béranger, addressing the couple who had been interned in Singapore, "only Buddhists are passionless and passive and do not believe in killing."

"While I was the prisoner of my fine patriotic countrymen, Kim killed the cow at Septeuil [the Bérangers' country house]," said Madame Béranger. "Kim is supposed to be Buddhist, *plus ou moins.*"

Kim lit his employer's cigarette and put a porcelain bowl of chicken on the silk chair in front of solemn, owl-eyed Sing Tow.

"Oui, madame, la religion de mon pays, de mes ancêtres, c'est le Bouddhisme."

"I will not permit my son to join the army," said the thin, white-haired man with some passion. "Look, there he sits, a great uncouth oaf who can hardly wait to put on a uniform so he will be better able to rape pretty girls and be given free tools with which to kill and make destruction."

"But father, if there are no armies, no policemen, who will protect the innocent and the helpless children? Who will rescue victims from dictators' ovens?" But his father was not listening.

"My son will be a knight in shining armor," continued the old man. "He will become the sort who seduces a different woman every night. In the daytime he will steal food from the children's mouths, brave man! He will save their lives so they may know the joys of starvation. All armies are the same; they attract the young, ignorant, and clumsy, who are soon transformed by battle into power-craving demons. Devils who want power over the weak, power to steal and mutilate and with which to inflate their bestial egos. Look at my great brave son, soon he would be such a man, except that he will never have my permission." The old man rose and left the room through the brocade-curtained door. After a decent interval Kim followed him with a cup of tea.

"Father is old and bitter," said the young man quietly.

"Il a souffert," said Madame Béranger, giving Sing Tow a piece of brussels sprout.

"You must of course join the army," said old Béranger to his young guest. Kim lit his master's cigarette. "Your father will never agree to it, but between fathers and sons there is always something. Yes, life goes on, and the wars, they go on, and as Christians say, 'so it shall be forever more.' "

"What do you know of war, what do you know of it, *mon vieux!*" His wife wiped the dust from a large cracked Rosenthal plate that was to be taken to the kitchen and filled with a new supply of *petits pains*. Her husband had spent most of the war years in the United States. His favorite abode had been the now defunct Lafayette Hotel in New York, where he was a well-known figure. When service was not immediately forthcoming, he would appear in one of the corridors and clap his hands, loudly calling, *"Les femmes de Lafayette, ou êtes vous?"* This immediately summoned every chambermaid and housekeeper within hearing distance.

"I shall join the army," said the young man gently, "and I will have my father's blessing. It is all just a question of time. I shall wait and persuade; I can be patient."

"The Christians have the heroic virtues of courage and energy," said Béranger. "The Buddhists have the patience and the endurance of eternity. But is it always a good thing to endure?"

"Sometimes, *mon vieux,* we can do nothing heroic and nothing courageous. We can only endure. To endure means to be able to continue without bitterness so that we do not become sick and crazy. Yes, it is the bitterness that is the worst of the human torments." Madame Béranger, with her husband's secretary-mistress, had been held hostage for many months by the Gestapo.

The Germans had wished to apprehend Malcolm Béranger, who was an agent for the Free French in exile.

At about this point in the conversation my husband and I decided to leave for a few hours of sightseeing and supper with friends. When we returned, far later than expected, it was shortly before midnight. In the foyer a dim light burned, and behind it fell softly on the silk-covered wall the silhouette of a life-sized bronze Kannon, to whose spirit Dogen's Eihei-ji is dedicated.

Everyone was still gathered around the table in the dining room, though it was hard to distinguish faces in the smoke-filled room. The young man was pacing quietly up and down. No one spoke, but Sing Tow was snuffling and wiping crumbs from his shoe-button nose, catlike, with his paw. Kim moved briskly about with blankets and pillows. An early summer rain fell quietly outside, and an occasional horn could be heard through a partly opened door that gave onto an iron balcony.

Two years later we made a second trip to France, this time in early September. Again we were invited by family friends, who asked us to spend a week in the fishing village and artists' colony of St. Briac-sur-Mer. The rocky coast of Brittany is windy; heavy fogs and extraordinary tides, which empty whole harbors in a few hours, are a peculiarity of the region. We visited an old castle in a fragrant field of yellow anise, and took long walks along the heather-wrapped cliffs. St. Briac, like many old European villages, has great bells that are rung for the various offices of the church. Sometimes the sound was all around us in unexpected places, in misty corners of the flowering fields or gardens. Before the sun rose, one was wrapped in its numinous waves. Awake or asleep, the impelling voice of the bells penetrated one's heart; it was not a sound for the ears alone.

One afternoon we were taken to the tiny studio of a woman

famous for her *incunables*. Each page of an incunable was carved from a separate block of wood that was inked and to which the artist then applied her paper. Thus had books been made in Europe before 1500. A few months each year, this artist shared her studio with a sister-in-law, whose specialty was enamel creations. In fine brushwork on a small porcelain sign that hung on the front door of their atelier were the words "Aux Emaux."

The creator of the woodblock-printed books, a large, tweed-clad lady with piercing black eyes and snow-white hair framing her cheeks, showed us her remarkable and probably unique volumes. Like certain illuminated manuscripts of the Middle Ages, each page was a tangle of words, plants, and insects, intricate and graceful. Each page lived and breathed: myriad forms sprouted, flew, crawled, or undulated from it with compelling exuberance. Only one who knew the life of each small growing or sentient phenomenon from within could imbue a flat surface with such vitality.

"I always use Japanese paper when I can get it," the artist said. "*C'est un papier vivant.* My pages come alive from this paper. Through it each form, each letter speaks to me."

We were shown a number of books, one of which was a Celtic tale by Roger Vercel called *Brocéliande.* It began:

> *Brocéliande, oui, c'était bien ainsi . . . une forêt en une lande: voici les masses sylvestres puissamment gonflées, l'élan des pins, la boule des chênes et des hêtres, les spectres blancs des bouleaux, le frisson argenté des trembles. Et voici la lande: les ajoncs et les genêts qui sont en or, bien qu'on l'ait tant dit, les ronces géantes tombant en guirlandes de lianes. . . . Or, il semble soudain . . . qu'il s'opère dans l'atmosphere, dans les choses, dans le temps même, un changement subtil; que la grande sylve se peuple de présences anciennes.*

Brocéliande! Yes, certainly it was thus . . . a woodland upon a heath: here are the sylvan masses deep and dense, soaring fir trees, spherical evergreens and beeches, white specters of birches, a silvery chill of aspen. And here on the heath: golden genista and gorse, just as it was so often said, and giant brambles falling into garlands of bindweed. . . . But suddenly it seems that a change is taking place. A subtle change is being wrought in the atmosphere, in everything about, even in time, and there appear to be ancient presences in the great wood.

Brocéliande, a land where time stood still: was it a fantasy in the realm of the never-never? Here in this village, where modernity was largely still a stranger, Brocéliande seemed paradoxically and numinously at hand.

"Madame," said the artist, "I will make a souvenir page for you," and she applied a large sheet of paper to an inked block on her work table. "You see it is Chartres, Chartres and the bells. The ringing towers of Chartres." The spires of Chartres rose through tiers of bells, interwoven in a mysterious and sublime unity.

"Bells are important," said the old woman. "It is important to listen to what the bells tell us."

"They seem to ask a question," I said.

"The question and the answer are the same, *ma petite fille*, just keep listening and it will become clear. The question is the answer, and the answer always a question, and so humanity will ever find it to be."

❧

A year or so after my marriage a very dear old friend, René Gues-Willer, with whom I always spoke French, said to me: *"Hein, ma petite, qu'est ce que tu vas faire avec ta vie?"*

"I am ever so happy," I told him. "Jack has given up the idea that I might evolve into a typical Teutonic wife who lives in the kitchen making pastries all day. I have my Russian lessons, my dogs, my books. Then just across the street is the Esplanade where we can all go together."

My friend René shook his head.

"It won't always do," he said. "Now you are young and your husband is indulgent. But many things could happen, and worst, perhaps when you are older, there could develop *l'ennui,* the biggest danger of all for the young women. *Et en plus, ma petite fille,* you drink and smoke too much. It is bad for the health. Listen to your old friend. [He was older than my father.] It is time for you to learn how to do something useful. I have decided to teach you how to teach a language, not as it is taught in colleges for reading and for study, but as I teach it at the Berlitz school, for conversation, and as a way to find oneself in a new perspective, a new point of view. We will start next week. You will get the pupils, five is a good number, and I'll teach you how to teach them French. The method can be applied to any language, as you know. I've taught it to instructors of six languages. This is the best present I can give you. One day you will think of your old René and say, 'The old fellow did a good thing!'"

My friend has been dead for many years, but still I am often reminded of the good karma that brought us together for the many hours of help and expert instruction I received from him. In those days, when foreign languages were usually pedantically taught and learned by rote, René Gues-Willer impressed upon me that really learning a new language is a kind of rebirth, an enlightening expansion of one's awareness. The most important result of my friend's generous help was that some years later I became a tutor of English for foreigners. First I was a volunteer for the International Institute of Boston, and later I was employed by the East Asia Program of Harvard University's Yenching Institute.

A passage from the *Sutta Nipata,* one of the Buddhist scriptures read in school, often passed through my mind during the years that I tutored elderly refugees from eastern Europe for Boston's International Institute: "This samsara [world of birth and death] is full of pain; birth is painful; old age is painful; disease is painful; death is painful; this is the noble verity of pain. But this pain in itself is not eternal. . . ."

One of my first pupils was an old Polish doctor, a charming gentleman in his eighties with kind eyes and a sensitive, aristocratic face. He had had his own small hospital in the Crimea before the advent of the Communist regime, when he fled with his wife to Germany. There he found quite a good job in a rest home, which he should never have left. In America he was offered only badly paid, menial work. He was too well educated and civilized to make friends among his rough, heavy-drinking, hunting neighbors, and he could not afford to indulge his love for music, as most concerts and the necessary transportation were beyond his means. However, the source of much of his distress was what he considered the callous and dehumanizing atmosphere of the large hospital where he earned his meager income emptying slop pails and washing floors.

"It is in the whole world famous, the hospital where I work. How can such things be? All over this sad world, people look to America and say, 'There is brotherhood, there all have opportunities and all can find dignity.'

"Two days ago came an old woman to the ward. She could not well understand English. She cried when they took away maybe her best clothes made into a ball and tied up with a string. Then no more was she a person. She went to bed, asked for her son and for the priest, but all people said they were too busy to do anything. I hold her hands. Then comes the young nurse and says in her bad peasant's Polish that that is not my job and I must leave the ward. So I must leave, though a person is dying alone there with much pain. Outside in the corridor the young nurses just stand about to gossip."

I inquired if such things did not happen in hospitals everywhere.

"*Tak,* yes, yes, everywhere they can happen. But in this hospital it happens because of no heart. In other countries there are circumstances which prevent people from being well treated. In this American hospital the doctors and nurses care about the wonderful machinery, the theories from their books, to find out things in the laboratories. For the person, the suffering person with pain, so often they just do not notice. Old people are lying in dirty beds covered with sores and the nurses are drinking coffee. They do not want to notice anything."

Something else bothered the old doctor: "Quite often I am called to the office of the woman social worker. I am busy, I wish to do my work carefully and well, so I do not have so much time to talk to her; also I cannot understand very much what she wants to tell me. Only I am hearing like a litany 'everyone's good,' 'social responsibility,' 'we are proud of' this, that, or I don't know what, and then 'services—services,' so on and on and on she goes."

"Probably she cannot help herself," I said. "She is just another victim of our so-called Protestant ethic. In America, such people cannot rest at night unless they are sure that they have justified their existence and that the world is persuaded that they are socially useful. They may really do something of use, or they may sit at a telephone and gossip all day, or perhaps some of both, but as long as others are convinced that they are useful, they are happy and sleep well at night. Maybe your lady lectures you because she is insecure and she sees that what she's doing is not making anyone very happy, not even herself. Therefore she must convince herself that all is as it should be."

"Yes, yes," he said, "it must be so, and if I were only younger I would adjust to it all in time. I would get a medical degree from the big machine. For some years I would work at making sick and painful many mice and poor thin old dogs from the street. Madame, to see some of the poor people in this so famous hospital is bad; to see the poor animals in the laboratories tries one's belief in a good Creator. After receiving an American medical degree," concluded the doctor, "I could try to accomplish something in spite of that special ethic which I don't remember hearing about in Germany, though I did meet some Protestants there."

In exchange for my English lessons, one of my pupils, an elderly White Russian colonel recently arrived from Egypt, offered to help me with my study of his language. Together we read the poetry of Lermontov and he translated difficult passages into French for me.

"We have many famous writers in Russian, madame," said the old man. "Why is it Lermontov, this sad, cynical man, who pleases you? You are still very young, you have a handsome young husband, and you live in a country full of opportunities."

The passionate half-Scottish poet, with his pessimism, his irony, his preoccupation with destiny, had replaced the Heine of my adolescent literary affections.

> "Under him streams the light blue water,
> Above him shines a ray of golden sun.
> But he, the rebel, awaits the storm.
> Perhaps only the storm can bring him happiness."
>
> (from "Parus")

"This seems to be the way with ambitious people, with idealists, and with history, too," I said. "Humanity cannot really live with peace and tolerance and reasonableness. Lermontov knew well the demons of boredom, of unrest, the spirit of turmoil."

"Ah, so it has always been for the young and strong, madame. I too, when I was a young soldier, was anxious to destroy many things which I could not or wished not to understand. Now that I am old and will live only for a very little time, I would like to create something. I want to make beautiful what has been discarded and what has been wasted in this rich country.

"Every week there comes the day of the trash barrels, I take an early morning walk—before five o'clock. In the barrels I find many things, many useful things, and all I put into my big sack."

He produced his findings: soapdishes, rusting cookie cans, plastic flowerpots, glass jars and bottles of all shapes and sizes. Many were dirty, and some still contained bits of dried food.

"Last month my wife and I went to Boston. A terrible trip, madame—so much noise, dust, and too many people! Together we went to the pawnshops and finally we have found one man to buy from us a brooch which was brought with us from Russia. Then we have taken that money and gone to a store for the arts, where we bought paint and the smallest, smallest brushes that were for sale. See"—and he showed me what indeed were tiny brushes, created for infinitely fine and detailed work—"I have never painted anything, madame, but now I will make beautiful every dirty thing which will support paint."

And paint he did: carefully repaired old furniture, bottles, boxes, and cans were covered with a profusion of flowers, and an occasional fruit or vegetable. Some he copied from nursery catalogues, some from botanical manuals (roots and all), and others from memories of the Ukrainian peasant art of his native Russia. In front of the prominently situated traditional icon of the Blessed Virgin, he placed a graceful yellow bottle, decorated with curious little flowering vines.

"It is the only one I make like that, and it is for God. God and the Blessed Mother know that flowers may come out in strange and unexpected times and places."

One afternoon my pupil-teacher made one of his rare telephone calls. His wife was dead, and there was to be a graveside funeral the following day. The old lady was to lie in a corner of a bare new cemetery a few miles from her last earthly home.

An aged, threadbare priest distractedly chanted the old Slavonic service, accompanied by the colonel. About eight or ten people were present, with two or three exceptions, members of the family. The ancient liturgy, timeless and numinous, had a spontaneity and simplicity that no conventional pietistic talk could approach in dignity or grace. At the end of the chanting, each of the participants in turn knelt and threw a handful of rain-soaked dirt onto the plain wooden coffin in a final gesture of communion and love. Everyone present, except for one very tall tweedy woman, joined in this traditional Russian expression of farewell.

About a week after the funeral I visited the colonel as usual for an afternoon of English and Lermontov. He brought me tea in one of the cups he had decorated himself. He was unusually agitated and did not drink any of his tea. Finally he said, "Madame, I wish very much for you to look at something." He rose, beckoning me to follow. Together we went to the cellar of the house. "Madame, here I have been busy since the funeral. I have made one last gift for my wife. You see, for the grave a stone is very expensive, and for now I cannot buy one. My daughter must save her money for the education of the children; education is so important in America. So I have made for my wife this—" and he carefully drew aside coverings on a workbench in the corner of the room. Under layers of gunnysacks and wrapping paper lay his handiwork, a three-foot wooden cross, carefully made and finished, and painted with hundreds of tiny flowers on a pale blue background. I noticed, as I had on a number of other occasions, that the old man's hands were stiff and swollen. Possibly he suffered from arthritis. I marveled that he was able to paint those many tiny flowers, which with time and practice were becoming ever more detailed and expert.

My friend was obviously pleased to have his handiwork admired, after which he covered it again carefully.

"There are six layers of varnish," he said, "and I shall put on more coats every few days for several weeks, then it will be able to withstand all kinds of weather."

During the next few visits I heard no more mention of the project. But one morning, very early, came a second unexpected telephone call, and this time a request to be driven to the graveyard within the hour; this was startling, as the old man never made any move that he had not planned in detail for at least a week in advance. He had never asked me to take him anywhere before, though he had several times accepted offers of rides on special occasions.

I arrived to find him pacing—it might be more correct to say marching—up and down the sidewalk in front of his house. When the car stopped, he climbed in without speaking. His face was white and taut. We drove in silence to the graveyard, where he asked me to wait in the car. He was gone for about half an hour. Worried that he was having trouble making himself understood and that he might be in need of his interpreter, I left the car and searched for him in the area where I was sure his wife had been buried. As I knelt down to inspect a small stone marker, a voice behind me that I hardly recognized said: "They have dared, madame, they have dared to desecrate a grave." He helped me to my feet with a surprisingly strong arm, and together we walked to the opposite side of the cemetery. The door of the large cement toolhouse was open and we walked in.

On top of a pile of dead flowers, broken discarded baskets, and grass cuttings was the last gift. I learned later that wooden monuments were not permitted in the cemetery. We carried it out to the car; it was unexpectedly heavy. On the ride back to his house he sat as staunchly erect as ever, his strong features immobile, though tears streamed down his white cheeks, and he made no effort to wipe them away. His lips moved, and though no sound could be heard, the words were unmistakable: *"Bogoroditzā Dēva, radonisīa"*—Mother of God, Virgin, be joyful. . . .

6 ASIAN CHRISTIANS, ASIAN BUDDHISTS

> *Life is like a sword that*
> *wounds, but cannot wound itself:*
> *like an eye that sees,*
> *but cannot see itself.*

Wakon yosai, "Japanese spirit and Western know-how": during the years I tutored Asian scholars for Harvard University's East Asia Program, I heard a great deal about this remarkable cultural phenomenon. I learned something about the ambivalence it created in the hearts and minds of Japanese people.

However, another aspect of the Japanese psyche particularly interested me, as it clearly paralleled a recent development very prominent among young Westerners disillusioned with the institutions and dogmas of their own tradition. Persuaded of the effective "instrumentality" of Eastern spiritual techniques, some Westerners feel their success, both worldly and spiritual, must depend on the choice of just the right Asian teacher, or just the right meditation technique. In the 1950s, Japanese scholars came to the West hoping to find gurus, roshis, to rescue them from themselves. Some favored charismatic personalities. Most were in search of a new spiritual and social persona, identified with what they worshipfully hoped would prove a more secure life than the one they believed had been destroyed by World War II. One bright-eyed latter-day samurai, who taught in a missionary establishment in Tokyo, catechized every Westerner with whom there was an opportunity for serious conversation with the question: "What is behind the wonderful dynamism of this Western civilization?" The expected ritual response was, of course, "The Protestant ethic." I am reminded of this enthusiastic gentleman when Westerners ask me if Zen isn't the source of all that remarkable Japanese energy, the force that has made possible Japan's postwar recovery as well as all those technological accomplishments.

One of my pupils, a solemn, ascetic Japanese professor who was a convert to Protestant Christianity, asked me to which sect of Christianity I belonged. When I replied that I was a Buddhist, persuasion was necessary to convince him that I was not indulging in some sort of American humor. He inquired how this was possible for such a traditional Bostonian; surely the tradition of my family must be Protestant! I replied by asking him about *his* family's tradition. He smiled and admitted: "Actually it is Buddhist. But," he added, "Buddhism has no special ethic with which one can transcend the evils of society."

"Well," I said, "there are the *Kai*—the Precepts."

"They have no social value; they are not a social ethic."

Then I read my Christian friend, who was very much interested in and preoccupied by the relationship of religion and history, the following historic letter.

September ye 15, 1682

To ye Aged and Beloved Mr. John Higginson:

There is now at sea a ship called the Welcome, which has on board an hundred or more of the heretics and malignants called Quakers, with W. Penn, who is the chief scamp, at the head of them.

The general court has accordingly given secret orders to Master Malachi Huscott, of the brig Porpoise, to waylay the said Penn and his ungodly crew, so that the Lord may be glorified, and not mocked on the soil of this new country with the heathen worship of these people. Much spoil can be made by selling the whole lot to Barbadoes, where slaves fetch good prices in rum and sugar, and we shall not only do the Lord great service by punishing the wicked, but we shall make great good for his minister and people.

Master Huscott feels hopeful, and I will set down the news when the ship comes back.

Yours in ye bowels of Christ,
Cotton Mather

"I have read some of the sermons of Cotton Mather. He was a famous New England theologian, whose father was once president of Harvard College," said the professor thoughtfully, "but I have never seen such a letter." And he thought about it for a few minutes. Finally he said: "Maybe it is impossible for most people, even for Christians, to transcend the evils of their own era. Perhaps the greatest wrongs and injustices of our own times await the discoveries and recognition of future generations. However, the Bible is an Oriental book. It was originally written for the Oriental mentality and it is in the lands of Asia where the Gospel will be preached as Christ wished. The Western mentality has perverted the pure teaching, and the Westerners have not the true religion of the Master."

I had only one pupil who was a convert to Roman Catholicism. He was a professor of English history at a Protestant university near Osaka. He considered himself to be an unusual phenomenon. "Usually," he told me, "Japanese Catholics only teach in Catholic universities." From one of my other pupils, a Protestant, I learned that the Catholic community in Japan was almost completely self-contained. "A Catholic not only sends his children to Catholic schools, but his doctor and dentist must be Catholics, too." One of my Buddhist pupils once remarked that in his university, a large national university, when the Catholic soccer team wanted to take on the Protestant team, a Buddhist was always found to be the go-between, as Protestants and Catholics could not speak directly to each other!

The Catholic professor was gentle and sweet-natured but a very firm traditionalist. His conversion, he told me, was stimulated, if I understood him correctly, by the collapse of the emperor's divine status after the war, and the Roman church seemed to afford the only sanctuary for one who felt that the primary need of both societies and individuals was a strong and ordered system with a dominant figure at the apex. In a few ways the professor was quite Westernized. His intellectual specialty was esoteric, especially for a Roman Catholic: Diggers, Levelers, Ranters, Agitators, and other sectarian efflorescences of the English Revolution. I discovered just how esoteric this Japanese scholar's researches really were when many years later I asked an Englishman, a Benedictine prior, to tell me about these seventeenth-century religious communities.

"They are mere names to me," said the august personage briskly. Obviously he was not interested in those idealistic countrymen of a bygone age. However, he was very much interested in their modern counterparts, the hippies. Like the hippies, the Seekers, the Levelers, the Family of Love, and other sectarian congregations had vigorously advocated free speech, tolerance, and egalitarianism without uniformity. In seventeenth-century England, where disputes over church government and the right to persecute were passionately debated, and where members of the established churches viewed free and tolerant discussion as absolutely sinful, the sectarians entertained the practice of questioning their preachers after their sermons or discourses.

Some years after his return to Japan, I visited the Japanese scholar of England's seventeenth-century religion, his home, family, and university. His wife was a beautiful and enchanting creature, an altogether beguiling personality, who looked a frail sixteen though she was the mother of four children, the oldest of whom was in high school. I was introduced only to the youngest offspring. He was a round Buddha-faced little person of about two years. In fact, he was one of the largest, most imposing two-year-old people I have ever encountered. His name was Jean-Baptiste Sebastian Dai Shin, or something equally remarkable.

"What will you do if he decides to be a Moslem, or possibly a latter-day Leveler or Agitator, when he grows up?" I asked his father. He laughed.

"Oh no, no, maybe that won't be possible. We are a very traditional family and he will want to follow our tradition, which is Catholicism," he replied. I wondered if he was persuaded that leveling and agitating were for history books, rather than a way of life that a person in any time, country, or family might get caught up in.

"When did your wife become a Catholic?" I asked him.

"When I was converted, of course, all my family and also our maid followed me into the church." His wife took from the sleeve of her elegant kimono her Catholic rosary and showed it to me. It too was a convert from Buddhism. The lady carried in her purse a number of tiny sachets whence emanated an incenselike scent. She held one out for me to smell.

"It is just like a Buddhist temple," she said. "It is my favorite fragrance. Beautiful, isn't it?" Her husband told her that his American tutor of English was a real curiosity, a Western Buddhist.

"How nice, oh, that is nice," she said. "And can you burn incense and chant *Namu Amida Butsu*? It is beautiful."

During one of my stays in Japan I was accompanied to a Buddhist temple in the mountains of Yokawa in Hyogo Prefecture by this hospitable professor and his wife. The professor had kindly procured a car from his university for the journey. We had tea together in the old country temple, and the professor was impressed by the young assistant to the old temple master.

"He is a very good person, I think. He is very humble and very respectful of his old master," said my professor approvingly.

After the tea we walked along one of the highly polished verandas that led to the courtyard and that also passed before the temple's Buddhist shrine. The sliding door was slightly open. The lady stopped before the partly opened door and looked in. Her husband walked on a few steps and then turned back when he realized that she was no longer following. She touched his elbow lightly: "Look, look," and she indicated the shrine. "Isn't it nice, isn't it pretty?" she said softly.

Her husband did not reply but guided her firmly to the veranda steps and their waiting shoes.

As they walked through the courtyard to the temple gate, the professor conversed with the temple master's assistant. Both had been students at Tokyo University. The professor's wife followed silently behind. In the palm of one hand was one of the little sachets, which, with her handkerchief, she occasionally held against her cheek.

A distinguished Korean scholar of Buddhist history had somewhat different reasons for his researches at Harvard. Though a Buddhist, he taught in a Christian college in Korea. He was also the college librarian, and financial resources for expanding the library were at his disposal. Much of his time in Cambridge was spent assembling mountains of material to be microfilmed.

"Someday my university will have the best library of Buddhist and Mongolian materials in Korea," he told me cheerfully. I inquired if many of the students in his Christian college in Korea were interested in Buddhism. The professor was amused. "Maybe not. But once every year comes the turn of each member of the faculty to talk in the Christian chapel. We must each of us give some talk, want to or not! Every year I talk about Buddhism and always afterwards, the president of the university visits me and says: 'Now next year you *must* talk about Christianity.' But each year, anyway, I always tell the students more about Buddhism. Maybe soon no more talks will be wanted from me. I am not sure, but I think this is the way it will turn out."

Shortly before his return to his home and country, my Korean professor brought me an interesting goodbye present. On four sheets of paper he had written in his elegant calligraphy what he called one of the most important of Buddhist scriptures: the Heart of Wisdom Sutra. This is a condensed but rather complete statement of much of the basic ontology of nearly all the Mahayana, or Great Vehicle, school of Buddhism. The sutra is chanted in monasteries and homes in the northern Buddhist countries, as well as in those parts of Southeast Asia where the Mahayana teaching is followed.

Nearly all of my adolescent Buddhist reading had been on the Hinayana, or Small Vehicle, form of Buddhism. This school of Buddhism presents the teaching of the Buddha as a rational philosophy and practical morality based on the Buddha's Four Noble Truths. These verities involve the origin and cure of suffering. The teachers of the Hinayana school maintain that realization of *anatta*, the unreality of self, is the heart of the matter and is attained by the practice of the following Eightfold Path: right belief, right resolve (to avoid sexual promiscuity, to harm no living creature), right speech, right conduct, right occupation, right effort, right contemplation, and right *samadhi,* or absorption in an enlightened state of mind.

Most of the first Westerners to explore or accept Buddhism were impressed with this basic scheme and interpreted it with literal and fundamentalist fervor. Here, some Westerners believed, was a religion of no-religion, a do-it-yourself psychology that could enable the energetic and intelligent to divest themselves of egotism and anxiety. Were the Buddhist way skillfully experimented with in the great laboratory of life, and mental, spiritual, and physical energy brought to bear, by his own efforts a man could expect to accomplish his salvation, Nirvana, or Nibbana as it is called in Pali, the canonical language of Theravada Buddhism. Until very recently, most Christian missionary writers also interpreted Nirvana according to this fundamentalist recipe. They believed Nirvana was annihilation. By contrast, these missionaries believed their Christianity to be a supernatural route to a positive goal, a paradise or a triumphant establishment of the kingdom of their God.

The nature of Nirvana, I discovered from my researches, was a subject of thorny debate among French, German, Russian, and English scholars of Buddhism. There were many conflicting interpretations of the nature of the great "Void,"* interpretations which, I decided, sometimes told one more about the mentality of the scholars involved than about the nature of the Buddhist ultimate reality. Was the Buddhist Nirvana simply extinction? Was the Nirvana of the Mahayana synonymous with the God and paradise of the Hindus or Christians, or was it something else? Did a man's interpretation and choice of a particular word and symbol for the ultimate reality actually influence his behavior?

Another question that I pursued with considerable interest was the relationship of the Hinayana form of Buddhism to the

*See footnote on page 108.

Mayahana. Most of the first Western scholars and adherents were persuaded of the superiority of the former because of an alleged compatibility with science. They maintained, and this some modern scholars do not accept, that all the Pali texts of the Small Vehicle were older and therefore purer than the scriptures of the Mahayana, which were composed in Sanskrit. The Mahayana, in its many forms, stressed the spirit rather than the letter of the Enlightened One's teaching. And could one say that an acorn is purer than its final evolution in the form of a large and flourishing tree? The Mahayana teaching, with its emphasis on faith and on the unity of all creation, and particularly with its stress on the Eternal Buddha, as well as the Buddha nature inherent in all creatures, proposes a universal salvation that over eons of time countless Buddhas and Bodhisattvas strive to attain. The best teachers of the Mahayana have always recognized the myriad ways to enlightenment, to the "homeless home." The value and depth of the Mahayana are progressively appreciated as, with age and experience, we discover the infinite complexity not only of the individual psyche but of the nature of so-called good and so-called evil in the world around us. However, I wondered, to what degree is human nature capable of selflessness and self-restraint? Inherent in self-delusion, I reflected, was a capacity to evolve ever more subtle manifestations. I remembered being told by someone that he knew of a supposedly enlightened Zen master who still had a ferocious temper even after nearly a lifetime of the practice of meditation. Was a Buddha, a truly enlightened man, a totally selfless being?

I put some of these questions to my Korean mentor. He simply laughed and said, "A scholar of religion has many big questions and many small answers." Nevertheless, I decided I must study the decoratively copied Heart Sutra with some care. I was full of what seemed to me to be big questions but I had no answers, not even small ones. My mentor did not seem unduly impressed by the pull-yourself-up-to-Nirvana-by-your-bootstraps versions

of Buddhism. He listened to my ruminations on their pronouncements and tenets patiently enough, but concluded, "Yes, yes,
it is very important for Buddhists to follow the *Vinaya,* the moral
precepts, at least as well as they are able, and for them to know
concentration, discretion, and tolerance. But if Buddhism were
only some kind of moralism, it would not be a religion, which,
of course, only means it might have too many limitations. In
true religion there must be a meeting place for everything, large
and small, and for all beings, good and bad, as well as the completely ordinary ones."

These were stimulating thoughts. The Hinayana Buddhism
of certain Western writers, I thought, possibly could lead to the
cultivation of an egotistical preoccupation with nonself and an
intolerant, puritanical rejection of the everyday world. My
mentor, on the other hand, did not seem to find that his religion
was in conflict with his love of books, of art or poetry, and above
all, of nature. As a descendant of the last reigning queen of
Korea, he had had a sophisticated education in the intellectual
and aesthetic traditions of both the Orient and the Occident. He
loved Western classical music and French impressionist painting,
as well as his own traditional Korean poetry.

I asked him to tell me something about the Heart Sutra, but
he only said, "Oh, I can't tell you anything about it, anything
important, that is. You have to understand it for yourself. If you
read some things, of course, it is useful, but in the end each has to
find the Buddha heart for himself. I don't know how to tell someone about finding it. It is a matter of karma and the inborn
Buddha nature. There is a kind of prayer that Japanese and
Korean Buddhists like. It is both beginning and end of the Buddha
Way, this vow of the Bodhisattva:

"*Pŏnno mujin sŏwŏndan:* Suffering is infinite, vow to alleviate it.

"*Chungsaeng mubyŏn sŏwŏndo:* Sentient beings are countless,
vow to enlighten them.

"*Pŏmmun muryang sŏwŏnhak:* The Dharma is infinite, vow to study it.

"*Pulto musang sŏwŏnsŏng:* The Way of the Buddha is endless, vow to follow it.

"This is a pointer, but it is also the heart of Buddhism. Now, there is an important part of the Heart Sutra, too. Western scholars call it magic, or perhaps they call it superstition. They do not understand the meaning or importance of this sutra's final words. They are," and he translated for me: " 'Gone, gone, completely gone over to the Other Shore. Enlightenment, *Svaha.*'

"You can't translate *Svaha* at all. You see, the words are simple, but they are also the most difficult to understand. Anyway, there is no need to translate them back and forth from one language to another. They are to be contemplated; contemplated and chanted during one's whole life. When the karma is right, that Other Shore appears, the shore so distant and at the same time as near to us as our own hearts. When we find ourselves on that Other Shore, then we are able to understand the great 'magic' of the sutra."

7 THE MAN WITH
THE BAMBOO TRUNK

From the heart
weary of noise and dust
a lark rises singing.
                    Takeo

Soen Nakagawa Roshi, poet, artist, and Zen master, and one of the most interesting Buddhist personalities in contemporary Japan, had been introduced to us by our friends the Robert Aitkens in Hawaii. In the spring of 1961, the roshi arrived in Cambridge dressed in traditional monk's garb and carrying an enormous trunk made of woven bamboo. Shortly after his arrival, as I was preparing my Western version of egg rice, he tied back his sleeves and made rice cakes with sweet, gooey red bean paste to put inside the traditional Japanese delicacy. At supper our black cat, Miko, sat in his lap and he fed her bits of shrimp and ice cream with his chopsticks. This endeared him to the Japanese Sanskrit scholar who was living with us that year. Professor Fujita and sleek, green-eyed Miko had a special understanding. She slept on his books and papers while he went on his bicycle to the fish market. They shared the special delicacies he brought home.

"This is a nice household," said the roshi. "I feel at home here."

The second morning of his visit, he suggested that we go to the Boston Museum of Fine Arts, "a museum famous in Japan."

"What kind of art do you like?" he inquired. I replied that I was most partial to Japanese screen paintings and to the French impressionists.

"Do you like Christian art?" he inquired.

"Many European artists who paint Christian themes seem to enjoy blood and cruelty, and then they combine all that with nakedness," I replied. "I find it a distasteful combination. Byzantine painting is different; there is wisdom and mystery in those solemn Byzantine faces."

When we arrived at the museum, the roshi steered us to a gallery of Spanish oil paintings.

"Now this is what you do not find lovely," he said thoughtfully, and he calmly studied a particularly harrowing picture of a saint being sadistically dispatched. "It is a strange mentality," he said, "all those many kinds of crucification. I have known Catholics in Japan, quite a few in fact. My brother and my brother's son went to Catholic universities. I asked my brother to study this mentality of Christianity and to explain it to me. But he could not do so. He only learned the way of business. He says that is what is well taught in Christian colleges and he cannot understand Christianity. He thinks it is only understandable for Christians, maybe only for Westerners. He is a traditional Japanese."

"Yesterday," I said, "when I went to buy the flowers that are in your room from the florist in Harvard Square, I saw a Japanese girl there and she wanted flowers for a special occasion in an Episcopalian church. I bought a Western-style bunch of flowers for you; she purchased only a few flowers to arrange in

Japanese style for the Episcopal church. Do you think either of us was being traditional?"

The roshi laughed. "No matter how flowers are arranged, never mind what tradition, they can speak quite plainly when the languages have nothing more to say!"

We stopped together in front of a life-sized and painfully realistic Crucifix. "Do you think that this speaks plainly when language has nothing more to say?" I inquired. The roshi shook his head.

"It says something, yes, but not plainly; what can it be that these Christians want, what can it be?" Couldn't it be different from what they think and believe they want? I reflected. Was it possible for anyone to be sure of his deepest desires? "The Church of Vienna," as a psychiatrist friend referred to Freud and his followers, did not seem to have evolved answers to questions of human motivation more persuasive than the rationalizations of the Christian dogmatists. Christianity and Freudianism, I thought, suffered from ontologies both limited and limiting.

After we had returned to the house the roshi produced several ink paintings from the bamboo trunk.

"These were done by an interesting friend of mine. Originally he was a painter of traditional Japanese *sumi* pictures. Then he became a convert to Christianity and he joined the Russian church in Tokyo. After ordination to the priesthood, he was sent to Russia for further training and there he learned to paint Christian pictures in the Russian style. When he returned to Japan he painted many Christian themes, many, many such pictures. But somehow he was not happy, in fact when we first met he was in the deepest despair. His spiritual questions were not answered, and he did not know what he should do. He asked for my advice, so I told him I thought maybe he should paint some bamboo: no more Christs, only flowers, clouds, and bamboo. He made many sheets of clouds, flowers, and bamboo; all over his studio were rice-paper sheets of them. He became a little calmer, I thought. Then I could suggest that he paint an ordinary man, just an ordinary poor hermit with nothing special about him." The roshi put some ink pictures on the rug and we looked at them together.

"What a strange face his hermit has," I said. "I prefer the clouds and flowers."

"Now," said the roshi, "when he became fairly calm with the painting of clouds and bamboo and the strange-faced hermit, I thought he should try to paint a Japanese kind of Christ. I told him he should paint a smiling Christ." Then the roshi pulled from a rice-paper wrapping still another painting.

"It's frightful, as depressing in a way as some of the things we saw in the museum today. Only, of course, the style is very different." The traditionally painted Japanese Christ was seated cross-legged and was smiling, to be sure; but the smile could only be described as a leer. The face was a death's-head, skeletal and empty.

"Yes," said the roshi, "there really is something the matter with that picture. Something is not right about it. My friend has more painting to do, he has not yet found what he is in search of and he must keep painting. Surely he will find what he is searching for, but it is a matter of time." I could not help being reminded of a book I had seen in a Swiss bookshop. It was entitled *Buddha Lächelt—Maria Weint* (Buddha Smiles—Mary Weeps)* and was by a German author of a number of volumes on the spiritual life. "It was not written of Christ," says this German Catholic, "that he ever smiled. . . . God's Son gave to the world tears of compassion, tears of sympathy, not a smile, remote and isolated from the sufferings of creation." Apparently a smiling Buddha, a smiling Christ, cannot be created by an artist who has not seen the world through the eye of his own Buddha nature.

*Ursula von Mangoldt, *Buddha Lächelt—Maria Weint* (Munich, Otto Wilhelm Barth Verlag, 1958).

Before his departure from Cambridge, the roshi produced some ink drawings from a very different source.

"Look," he said, and spread sheets of rice paper around the hearth. "On these papers is only one figure, one Compassion Bodhisattva about one hundred times on each sheet." The figures were all the same, a remarkable uniformity. However, if scrutinized it was possible to see that each figure, so deftly done, was different in some way from all the others. Each was unique and, tiny as it was, had a special strength, a particular vividness.

"The lady who painted these few sheets which I am showing you here has in recent years made many many thousands of only this one Bodhisattva of Compassion. When first I met the lady she was a young girl, recently crippled by a dreadful disease which destroyed her ambition and opportunity to become a ballet dancer after the Western fashion. Her parents were in despair because their daughter had become like a vegetable, and I was called to talk to her. Of course, I did not know what to say to such a young woman, but to please her parents I went to visit, and with me I took a calligraphy brush and rice papers. I drew for her one Compassionate Bodhisattva—then another, and then after that some more. Her eyes followed what I was doing and when I saw her interest, I took her hand and guided it until she was able to draw this figure by herself. Over and over she painted, and at each visit I told her what she had done was fine but she must do many more. She must do twenty-five in a day, then fifty, then a hundred, and so on like that until she was doing many hundreds each day.

"That was many years ago. Now she is a happy woman. She still draws the same figure, but she can draw many other things, as well. She has talent; but most important, she has discovered that this Bodhisattva, whom she has drawn so many thousands of times, lives in her own heart, as well as in the hearts of others who are not awakened as she is. She has kept careful count of the number of pictures she has made. I told her each must be counted, that it was very important not to forget even one single figure. So on every page is written the exact number of Bodhisattvas she has drawn. The counting, the attention is good; one should see each thing as it is in itself in order to experience complete Buddhist awakening.

"However, it is not the counting which is most important. Counting or not counting is not the point. What matters is for each person to discover the Buddha heart in himself or in herself. It is the discovery of the Buddha heart that really matters," the roshi concluded.

The ink-brushed mantra, like a mantra that is chanted or that is simply absorbed during silent contemplation, reveals its deepest meaning in the course of lifelong practice. "What is important is the Buddha heart!" Nakagawa Roshi repeatedly tells his pupils in reply to their queries about Zen training and practice. Sun Buddhas and Moon Buddhas are not created by techniques of concentration, and they do not dwell in a never-never land of the imagination. They are to be found in the ordinary everyday world, in awakened hearts.

As this book is being written, some twelve years after the above conversation took place, a large rough stone is being engraved with a reproduction of the two-millionth ink drawing of the Bodhisattva of Compassion. This ink drawing was specially created several feet in height, and the stone on which it is being reproduced will be placed in the garden of Ryutaku-ji, Nakagawa Roshi's temple.

Later in the spring of 1961, I set off for my third journey to Japan. I planned a stay of about two months, during which I would take part in the zazen retreats of temples of both the Rinzai and Soto schools.

"You will get very tired, I think," Roshi had said, "so between temple visits you must get some rest and proper food with my brother's family. They live in our most traditional Japanese Buddhist way in a suburb of Tokyo. Perhaps this will be the first time you have lived with a Japanese family."

I left Boston by plane for Tokyo, where I was met at Haneda airport by Nakagawa Roshi, his brother and sister-in-law, and their son, the roshi's nephew.

"Elsie-san, here we are. Look up!" It was the roshi's familiar deep voice. Smiling and waving on the observation platform above was the whole family. A small bunch of spring flowers landed on my shoulder; they had been tossed by the tall nephew in his dark student's uniform. After my baggage had been collected, the roshi turned to me: "Will you come to Ryutaku-ji tonight? Are you ready to start zazen right away?" Actually I was very tired, and though I had been practicing zazen quite intensively for about four years, I was not able to use it as a substitute for sleep, as some practicants claim is possible. However, it was obvious that the roshi had his own plans, so I said that I was willing to start anything wherever and whenever he wished.

The roshi's brother found a taxi, and into it I climbed with the roshi and the pleasant young nephew, who spoke quite good English. It was after midnight; the drive to Ryutaku-ji was to be of about four hours' duration, Shizuoka Prefecture being about a hundred and fifty miles distant and the roads in very poor condition.

Conversation with the roshi's young nephew was interesting and lively. He told me about his school, his books, and what he read in the newspapers about "abroad." Then followed a stream of inquiries about life, especially about student life in America. The roshi listened quite intently for a while, but finally he remarked that the traffic noises were unpleasant. He produced ear plugs, which he duly installed in both ears, and within minutes was peacefully asleep, sitting cross-legged on the car's narrow seat.

Somewhere beyond the resort town of Atami, the taxi was forced to a halt in a long line of trucks and trailers. The narrow bypass permitted passage of traffic from only one direction at a time, and an hour's wait was necessary before the taxi could proceed. The driver made a few complaints. Workers high above us were still drilling and digging, and every few minutes a shower of stones and dirt fell against the side of his car. The car seemed to be the object of his concern; he was obviously wide awake and not at all disturbed by the late, or I should say early, hour.

Like many Japanese taxis, the vehicle was furnished with a colorful feather duster and live flowers suspended in bamboo tubes. The Japanese put flowers in what Westerners usually consider unlikely places, such as automobiles, elevators, and toilets. I stuck my finger into one of the bamboo vases, which was hanging just beside my head. Yes, it actually contained water.

At about three o'clock in the morning, the taxi arrived in Mishima village in Shizuoka Prefecture. At the bottom of the hill on which Ryutaku-ji stood, the taxi stopped and we got out and stretched our tired legs.

"Come," said the roshi, "we must climb the hill and Elsie-san must be very careful not to stumble or fall. There are many stones, and she has tall and thin-heeled shoes." There was no light on the path, and the road was steep.

"Are you getting tired?" asked the roshi as we picked our way up the path.

"I can't see where I'm going, I can't see you; in fact, I can't see anything at all," I said.

"That is the way it is, that is indeed the way things usually go. However, if you look above your head (you must not look down) you will see between the tops of all the high trees that there are stars. In dark, unfamiliar places one should always follow the stars. The path here is quite wide. Follow the stars and you will stay on the path." He was right. The stars were out in great bright clusters and indicated the way between the black silhouettes of the treetops.

I heard footsteps approaching us from a distance.

"Ah," said the roshi, "we are being met. The person who comes is the man with the kindest heart in this temple." A disembodied voice greeted the roshi in Japanese. A strong, rough hand gently but firmly took my small suitcase from me.

"The voice that you heard just now, the presence that could not be seen in this dark night, belongs to the man who has the kindest heart in our sangha community of Ryutaku-ji. Only he would come out at this time to carry suitcases and to arrange the bath, and all this though no one has asked him."

"Is he a monk?" I inquired.

"He is a kind of lay monk," said the roshi. "He has been in this temple quite a few years now. The story of how he came to the temple is rather interesting, I think. When he was a small boy of about eleven years of age, he heard the song of a cicada. The sound came from inside a garden wall past which he was walking one day. This was a beautiful sound, he thought, and he wished to find the wonderful small creature that made it. So he climbed over the wall and searched for the insect inside the private garden which lay on the other side of the barrier. For this act of trespassing, he was sent to jail. While imprisoned, he learned the profession of the pickpocket. For many years, he was engaged in this activity, and thus was many times inside the jail, then outside it, and then back inside again. While living in prison he enjoyed many hours with the reading of haiku poetry, including, so he told me, one volume which I wrote a long, long time ago. After that last time in jail, he decided that he would visit me here at Ryutaku-ji. He only wished to tell me that while sitting so many long hours in his cell he liked the reading of my haiku poems. So we talked awhile. Then finally he asked if there was something he could do here in this beautiful Ryutaku-ji. You see, he was still in search of beauty. He has been living here ever since that day. He loves the country, this Mishima, its trees and variety of flowers. He knows just how to take care of vegetables, flowers, and bushes. If you go to the woods, to the fields, and find any kind of plant, he will always know its name and what are the special characteristics."

When we arrived within the temple gates, the roshi vanished into his quarters, and his nephew pointed out the visitor's bath. Once undressed inside the steaming bathhouse I slipped into the water, which had been cooled to accommodate a non-Japanese skin. I sat in the large wooden tub, into which a kind hand had strewn camellia flowers. The camellias and the tired visitor steamed together in the dimly lit bathhouse. The sound of the early morning peace was absorbed by the floating flowers.

I remained in the temple for about a week. The roshi's old mother often invited me to her tiny house, which was located on the edge of a large field, a short walk from the temple. She was a widow and lived in that special combination of simplicity and elegance that is characteristic of traditional Japan. Possibly nowhere else in the world does elegance flourish not in spite of but because of poverty, nor is simplicity so dignified and graceful. Mrs. Nakagawa's tiny house was spotlessly clean; the tatami smelled of summer. Her black kimono was lined with soft green and pink silk. She was an accomplished cook and produced all manner of beautiful vegetable dishes for me, her son having told her that I was to participate in Tokudo and that I should no longer eat meat. A large glass of milk always awaited me at my place, "so you won't get sick," said Roshi.

On my return to Tokyo, I was invited to stay with the roshi's brother and sister-in-law in Shinagawa Ward, a vast, sprawling district with densely populated narrow streets. My host and his family were cheerful, hospitable people, and I was given the host's tiny study as a bedroom. Sometimes before I went to sleep I lay in the traditional futon sleeping quilts looking up at the titles in the bookcases, which began at the floor and ended up by the ceiling. There was an assortment of foreign books that included Hegel, some German histories, chemistry textbooks, several Dickens novels, and a Bible.

"Have you read much of the Christian Book?" I asked my host one day.

"In the university we had some courses, but I have forgotten everything now."

"Did you enjoy reading it?" I inquired.

"Well, of course it is supposed to be an important Western book . . ."

"Some Westerners are persuaded that if it is placed in every hotel room in the world, people will be converted to Christianity."

"In Japan," said my host's son, "there are certain objects that are thought to have special power; the power could even be in a book."

"But," said I, "Christians think the magic is in the stories the Bible tells. They believe in the Bible, a kind of magic maybe. They believe so deeply themselves that they think if other people just read their book they will believe and feel about it as believers do."

"Magic has a kind of simplicity," said Mr. Nakagawa. "The stories in the Bible have no order, no clear direction. There are always battles, confusions, and the god who is supposed to have created all those many quarreling men and women is dissatisfied with what he himself has made, but he is not powerful enough to make peace or harmony. He is not strong enough or quiet enough to bring peace or happiness to those creatures made from his own clay, made like him. So all are doomed to eternal duality—no *isshin*, oneness! A kind of hell, we think. Then there are so many strange names. Do the people in the hotels feel happier after reading about quarrels and about a god who cannot smile? Of course, with the Japanese television, there is now a great fad for the tales of the samurai of old. As in the Western Bible, many shouts and swords! Lots of people like that, too. They do not want peace or harmony, they want excitement."

Each morning when I awakened in this interesting household, it took a few minutes to recollect that I was indeed in Japan and on the floor of my host's study. In this neighborhood of houses with paper-thin walls, everyone woke up at once, in a wave of coughing, spitting, barking, meowing, crying, and staccato chatter. The first face I saw after I became conscious shortly after dawn was a dour countenance in a heavy Western-style gold frame. It was the face of the German clerical teacher of Mr. Nakagawa. The teacher's huge photograph hung at a slight angle, and I never failed to find myself within the range of his lugubrious gaze when I was horizontal on the futon quilts. "Japanese people are in the thrall of the teacher," someone told me once. Indeed, this teacher was certainly well placed to hold sway over his disciples. The top of the picture frame was almost flush with the low ceiling, and the Face dominated the room.

" '*Guten Morgen, meine Herren.*'

" '*Guten Morgen, Herr Professor.*'

" '*Und so,*' " Mr. Nakagawa continued, imitating the professor's voice in German, " 'today we have with us Kitagawa, Nakagawa, and Tanigawa: in other words, Mr. North River, Mr. Midstream, and Mr. Valley Stream. Then on the other hand we have Kawamura and Kawatake, Kawaguchi and Kawakami: that is, *Herren* River Village, River Bamboo, Estuary, and Upriver.' He loved the analysis of our names, my teacher did."

The Nakagawas, on learning that we had a black cat in Cambridge called Miko, were greatly amused.

"And how did she get such a name?" they wanted to know. A *miko* is a female shaman sometimes attached to a Shinto shrine. Like fortunetellers, they are rather good at telling people just what they want to hear, in return for which they sometimes manage to become quite wealthy.

"Well," I said, "she is very clever. She always knows how to ingratiate herself and how to get exactly what she wants from us, the most expensive tuna fish, the softest pillow."

"We love cats, too," said Mr. Nakagawa as his wife produced a family album in which there were pictures of their cat of sixteen years. "When she died we took her to a special temple where the priest chants sutras for animals, and she is buried behind the temple in a fine box on her favorite pillow."

"What was her name?" I inquired.

"She was called Mary."

"Mary?"

"We called her Mary because we hoped so much she would be the kind of virgin who miraculously gives birth only once. However, I am sorry to say that the births took place several times a year and our Mary had large families. It was hard for us in our small house, those little cats everywhere; in the bookcase, in the kitchen, in the cupboards, all over the house, wherever you stepped, were jumping our Mary's many little incarnations. Mary kept us busy, sometimes we were very tired. Where oh where to find new homes? Japan has many people, yes, but even more is the population of cats. But we loved that Mary very much indeed, and when she died we all shed tears and wept when we took her to the temple to be buried."

After about a week I bade goodbye to this charming and hospitable family. I was to return to Ryutaku-ji in order to take part in a special week-long zazen practice called sesshin. I gathered my possessions, pencils, bobby pins, and postcards from under the furniture and packed my two bulky suitcases. Before my departure I made a gassho to the spirit of the study, the bearded clerical Face in the big gold frame. At the doorway I put on my cold, damp shoes and followed Mr. Nakagawa down the narrow street, in which flowed a veritable sea of sentient life: delivery boys, toddlers, housewives, dogs, and cats.

I was alone when I journeyed the second time to Mishima village and the temple of Ryutaku-ji. I made the trip via Kyoto, and since the train ride was a long one, I decided to risk the extravagance of a first-class seat. It happened that I was one of the few women in a car full of businessmen. In Japanese fashion, the gentlemen all undressed themselves down to their long Japanese underwear and settled in their seats to enjoy the journey. I found it a trifle unsettling to be hurtled through the countryside, surrounded by men in the process of divesting themselves of their clothing. Nevertheless, the practice is obviously a sensible one, as the suits can be donned at the end of the trip free from creases and coffee stains.

At Mishima I found a taxi with great difficulty. When I asked several drivers to take me to Ryutaku-ji they stared coldly and drove off without a reply. I produced a large-denomination yen note, which I thrust at the last available driver even before making my request. He took my bag through his window and opened the passenger door. However, the prospect of the drive to the temple did not seem to please him in spite of the generous advance tip. Some time later, when I described this experience to Mr. Nakagawa he laughed and said, "The country people do not like to go to the temple after dark. They are afraid of spirits; it is the graveyard that makes them so nervous. About a year ago, one of the farmers in the region saw what he was certain was a ghost. Actually, we think it was a Westerner then staying at Ryutaku-ji. This visitor, a lady from Czechoslovakia, liked to take walks on the hot summer nights. She wore a white sari brought from India, for coolness, I suppose, and sang strange songs which sounded ghostlike to the simple farmer. So he fled in terror."

The taxi ride from the small country station took about three-quarters of an hour. It was nearly ten o'clock, and in the black starless night, clouds of mist wafted languidly through the dull beam of the automobile lights. The car drew up at the foot of the path to the temple. I fished around in my purse for the fare. When I handed it to the driver, he threw my soft zipper bag out of his window, a startling gesture, and when I climbed out after it, I had hardly closed the door before the car was off with screeching tires in a cloud of dust. A tiny lamp on a post indicated the foot of the path, and fortunately my bag had fallen just under it or I might have had to wait for the following morning to find it.

I picked my way slowly and carefully up the hill, looking above my head for a star or two above the tall treetops. None was to be seen anywhere. The path was covered with loose stones, and though I had anticipated this walk and had worn low-heeled shoes, the temple seemed impossibly distant. Several times I hit my ankles against the sharp stone curb that lined the path, and a wayward branch slapped my face in what seemed an unfriendly reception. Out of breath and discouraged, I decided to sit down for a few minutes to nurse my sore ankles and scratched face. I took a large step in what I thought was the direction of a distant curbing. I had not judged the distance well, and I stumbled over a small stone fence, landing in what seemed to be a hole about two feet deep and about the same number of feet wide. I sat there for a few minutes before the thought occurred that this hole in which I had fallen would probably be just about the right size for a burial urn. The path to the temple, as I had re-marked in the daytime, was lined with the graves of monks and abbots of the temple. I wondered, Is this where the old retired abbot, who is rumored to be dying, is to be planted?

These passing thoughts should have been disquieting, but I was curiously undisturbed. The night was still; I could feel the spring mist around me like a soft sponge against my face. I was quite unreasonably at peace. A rustling from somewhere behind me, and a warm furry presence pushed against my arm. It settled down there, indicating no desire to move or to be moved. The trees and bushes rustled gently; the warm-coated being and I were not alone. There were also unseen, bloodless presences, but they too seemed at peace. How curious it is, I thought, that all is really just as it should be. Everything has such an unreasonable and incomprehensible rightness about it, but this remarkable rightness is almost never apparent, though children sometimes sense it fleetingly. How effervescent, this heartwarming intuition! I sat there in a hole in the old Japanese graveyard and forgot my barked ankles and stinging face for what seemed a very long while, though probably it was only about fifteen or twenty minutes. The four-legged creature, possibly a large rat, decided to move on, and its departure made sharp, crackling sounds in the dry leaves and twigs. Refreshed and encouraged, I picked myself up and somehow managed to climb back onto the path and continue my way through the night up to the sleeping temple.

A Zen Buddhist sesshin, or retreat, is a time in which to "collect the thoughts," a literal translation of the word "sesshin." Actually the process involves focus and penetration, not really of thought, but of the nature of the mind itself. Retreats are conducted differently according to various temples or teaching traditions, and the retreats given especially for lay people usually involve less formalism and rigor than the retreats for young monks in training to become priests. Special temples for the discipline of young men who are only temporarily monks exact a military type of discipline that I feel is not always suitable for lay people, or for women. A friend once described a small Zen nunnery she had visited with the famous Zen philosopher Daisetz Suzuki as inhabited by the most unappealing and masculine women she had ever had the misfortune to encounter.

Retreats take place monthly, or used to, at Ryutaku-ji. Lay people are allowed to attend if they have had some zazen experience and if there is enough space available. Men sit in the regular meditation hall for the daily fourteen hours or so of zazen.

Women sit together in an adjoining shrine room. The time not spent in meditation is devoted to sweeping, thrice daily ceremonies of chanting, and three silent communal meals.

At the first sesshin breakfast at Ryutaku-ji, I discovered the stinging hot apricot pickle that Japanese people break into small pieces and mix with their rice. Unwisely, I popped the whole thing into my mouth at once and thought that I had consumed a small fire bomb, which proceeded to explode somewhere in midjourney to my stomach. Tears rolled down my face, and I hastily consumed as much rice and hot water as possible to temper the discomfort of that fiery morsel.

In the small shrine room adjoining the large meditation hall, I sat cross-legged in meditation with four other women, three Japanese and an elderly German from Los Angeles. She was a dressmaker by trade and always had a few dressmaker's pins on the white lace collar of her old-fashioned dress. We sat on the floor. She sat on a straight-backed wooden chair. Two of the Japanese ladies were young and elegant. They were dressed in black kimono with sleeves coyly lined with red stripes, over which were tied full-length black pleated skirts called *hakama*. They were obviously used to doing zazen, and they accomplished all the necessary motions of rising, bowing, and being reseated with grace and dignity. Their beautiful faces were immobile, unreal: like dolls in a shop window, I thought, but not without envy, as my swollen legs and aching back made me clumsy and graceless by comparison. They appeared not to notice the awkward foreigner except to hiss occasional instructions in Japanese, such as, "It is time for *sanzen* [private interviews with the roshi]. The men go first; we are always afterwards." Or "Tell the old woman she must always have her eyes open during zazen! Tell her to keep her legs together." The fourth member of our group was a gentle, round-faced girl, probably in her late twenties, who sat Japanese-style on her heels, as she had no long hakama skirt to cover her legs. Unlike the dainty, doll-faced creatures, she had warmth and a sweet expression. When the elderly dressmaker succumbed to a severe nosebleed on the third day of sitting, this kindhearted girl responded to the situation with the greatest possible solicitude. She helped the old woman to rest on the tatami floor and then fetched a bowl of cold water. In this she immersed a number of doll-sized handkerchiefs, with which she then wiped the old lady's nose and forehead. An hour or so later, the elderly woman was seated on her straight-backed wooden chair again, prepared to persevere into the wearying depths of her own psyche in a renewed search for enlightenment.

The first time I went in turn to Nakagawa Roshi's room for the required sanzen interview, he asked: "Are you uncomfortable maybe? Where?" I replied that I was nothing but one large ache, inside and out. "To ache makes the world black and ugly, and me just nasty!"

"Then," he said, "you must penetrate further into *Mu** or, if you would prefer it, God." And the roshi demonstrated what he meant with a long forceful exhalation that seemed to pull the word down into the innermost regions of the viscera. Then he rang his little bell, which signaled the end of the interview.

Mu, Mu, Mu, ache and irritation: the world pressed in on me painfully, unpleasantly combining irritation and discomfort. The doll-faced ladies were obviously at ease; they never moved a muscle except during rest periods, when they daintily patted their faces with tiny paper towels. I felt that should I not explode, I could not possibly survive the disagreeable thoughts and sensations, the emotional and psychological bile that arose from rarely recognized depths. Such sequences often began with a

---

Mu is the Japanese pronunciation of a Chinese ideograph that is usually translated as "Emptiness" or "Nothingness." This Nothing, which is pregnant with every possibility and is the "storehouse of the seeds of consciousness," is the source of the Buddha spirit. It is perhaps best described for Christians in the words of the *Theologia Germania:* "That which is perfect is called nothing." The Tibetan Buddhist saint Milarepa speaks of the awareness of the Void as "limpid and transparent, yet vivid."

"What am I doing here?" sort of emotion, an almost crippling malaise which arose from depths well below the functioning of the cerebral processes. Boredom, frustration, and mild paranoia followed in all-permeating waves. These had one uninspiring advantage: they created a distraction from the maddening and inescapable pains in my back and legs. A large insect crawled slowly but purposefully from the tatami to my skirt and thence onto my arm—his shiny black body loathsome, his eyes hatefully malevolent. I had always been afraid of insects, which of course is only another way of saying I disliked them. Mu . . . Mu . . . Mu . . . time stretched before me, an endless and suffocatingly narrow black funnel. The insect's shining, pitiless eyes were eviscerating me. No pity, no escape.

"My nature is black and ugly!" I told the roshi in the next interview. "I detest bugs, especially the big ants that live in your tatami. I dislike humanity and myself even more. I've never had so many hateful thoughts all together at once."

"Mu, Mu, God." The roshi's voice came from the depths of his being. Back in the meditation room, somehow I did get further into that Mu. It was frightening and black; I heard and saw nothing for what was probably a short period but seemed an eternity. Finally the light returned, the straw-matted floor undulated, and the oppressive mood vanished. My legs seemed remote; suddenly a bird's bright song, like the chime of a brass bell, broke into the room. It was overwhelming, that song; the bird must have been a messenger from paradise.

In the next sanzen, I said: "A bird sang from paradise!"

"Mu, Mu!"

On the fourth night, my turn at sanzen did not come until nearly ten o'clock.

"Are you all right?" asked the roshi as I stumbled in clumsily, making the ritual prostration.

"I'm just not real any more. Tomorrow I think I shall be dead," I replied.

"Go to bed," he said. "Go to your room and stay there very quietly, as there are others to come to sanzen and they must pass your door to come up here. Remember, your zazen must still continue and you must remain absorbed in Muuu!"

My bedroom was just below the roshi's sanzen room. I went there quickly, quietly closed the sliding door, and lay down on the futon quilts. I was asleep within a few seconds. Suddenly I was startled into wakefulness. From upstairs, from the direction of the sanzen room, came a great guttural shout, a Kabuki sort of shout, I thought later. There followed loud bumpings and thumps, then a falling body—a heavy one. The roshi's stick could be heard, no doubt on the back of some hapless monk wound up in the sticky tendrils of his koan.

"Well," I thought, reflecting on my own state of mind earlier in the day, "that is what is meant by the legendary stories about Zen monks getting whacked about by the master. It just gets too black and sticky on the way down to the bottom of the mind; such an explosion is just the koan working itself out."

The following day as we sat in our places, the sliding windows wide open to let in the spring breezes and an assortment of spring insects, an extraordinary phenomenon appeared and filled the small entrance to our room. Even the doll-faced girls stared in amazement for an unguarded moment or two. A figure over six feet tall and dressed in the long black robes of a wandering pilgrim peered down at us. In his right hand was a tall staff with little jangling rings at the top; under his left arm he carried a large meditation cushion of dark brown velvet. He had long white hair, a white beard, blue eyes, very pink cheeks, and was unquestionably a Westerner. He started to mount the step, evidently prepared to join us. In midstep, his form suddenly receded. Behind him stood the roshi, about half his height, who had caught him by the back of his robe and extracted him before he could enter our segregated company.

"No, no," said Roshi in a firm voice. "That way." And he indicated the hall where chanting ceremonies were held. Apparently the formidably bearded prophet was considered something of a distraction in the meditation hall, his behavior being somewhat eccentric, so that his meditation was to be carried on alone.

Nakagawa Roshi later told me his story. This curious man, from a first-generation Jewish family that had immigrated to California from Russia or Poland, had led an uneventful youth. He married and settled down to an existence that was conventional enough until well past middle age, when he discovered Buddhism. Aspiring to the "homeless state," he sold his house and, leaving his family, wandered pennilessly around Asia. He finally took to begging for food and lodgings from Buddhist temple masters, who were not always happy to receive him, as he was argumentative and he kept them from their work, or possibly from more agreeable activities. One day, sick and hungry, he arrived at Ryutaku-ji. Kindhearted Nakagawa Roshi gave him food and lodging, then kept him until his strength had returned. But finally came the moment when the pilgrim had to be gently evicted, as he was a distraction to everyone. He had no capacity for self-discipline, was untidy and lazy, and could not adjust to the rigors of life in a Zen temple.

Several times a year he returned to Ryutaku-ji, and always the roshi permitted him to remain for a time. One of these visitations took place in December. After a few weeks, the roshi informed him that the visit must soon be terminated.

"But where shall I go, Roshi?" the wanderer inquired.

"Maybe you should make a pilgrimage to Hokkaido," said Roshi. "Go on foot; you should walk even though it will be a long hard journey, and I think you will learn many interesting things." So the pilgrim, staff in hand, set off for this cold northern island of Japan. The trek to the north lasted about a month, the wanderer as ever making generally unsuccessful endeavors to insinuate himself into the lives of busy, conventional temple families.

Finally, one cold snowy night, he found himself completely without funds and with no place to sleep. As a last resort he requested shelter, late that night, in a small Buddhist nunnery. The nuns were old, they were nearly as poor as the pilgrim, and they had in their charge more orphans than their destitute establishment could adequately support. However, they allowed the homeless man to sleep in a corridor, for which he was deeply grateful, though the roof of the building leaked and cold drops of water seeped through cracks in the wood and fell onto his head all during the night. The following day, after a meal with the children, he left and walked to the center of Sapporo city. It was still snowing. Feeling quite at a loss as to what to do next, the pilgrim seated himself in a conspicuous place near a railway station, his empty wooden bowl before him, and began to chant Buddhist dharanis that he had learned by heart during his wanderings. No one paid any attention for some time. However, several hours after darkness had fallen, a sympathetic woman put a small-denomination yen note into the wooden bowl.

The wanderer spent the night on the pavement, and the following morning he resumed the cross-legged position and chanted. The snow drifted around him and collected on his head; people gathered about. They put money in his bowl and in his lap. A shopkeeper brought a small food offering and placed it before him, as well as a large bamboo container for the contributions of paper yen, which were beginning to blow about the sidewalk. By then the pilgrim had entered a sort of trance, and he stopped chanting neither to eat nor to sleep. He remained thus for four days; the chanting was stopped only for a few hours each night. At the end of the four days he rose, picked up his treasure, which by then was considerable and filled several large bamboo baskets.

"I was a rich man, really rich," he told the roshi. "But then I began to think to myself, What shall I do with this money? I want only to be free to wander where I please, and if I had money it would be something extra for me to carry around. Then I thought of those old nuns and of their thin pale children under the leaking roof. Now, I thought that was the place for which Buddha and karma had destined my baskets of money." Needless to say, the nuns and their charges were quite overcome with this good fortune.

"Roshi," said the pilgrim, "it was the happiest day of my life. Those nuns and children, crying and bowing, nothing like that ever happened to me before: to me, Emmanuel. I was the cause of some people being so beautifully happy and grateful. It was the blessing of Buddha." The inhabitants of the small temple had reason to be happy. Thousands of yen had been stuffed into the baskets, and not only was the temple roof repaired, but enough money remained to buy warm clothes and quilts for the orphaned children.

The only occasion on which I had an opportunity to meet and observe Emmanuel was the morning of my departure from the temple after the sesshin. We sat together in the roshi's small room. The roshi drew from a box an enormous frosted cake.

"One of the patrons of this temple has brought us this beautiful cake, which she has carefully made for me herself. Now we shall all have a piece." The roshi produced a small jackknife, a spoon, and some paper napkins.

"Oh," said Emmanuel, "that is much too rich for me. I'm not accustomed to such luxurious fare."

"Too bad, indeed," said the roshi. "This cake must be delicious. I plan to eat a large piece myself. The lady who has made such a beautiful sweet would certainly be disappointed should her efforts not be appreciated." But the roshi's train of thought was lost on Emmanuel, who was more interested in prospects for his next pilgrimage, which was to take him to Southeast Asia.

As it turned out, it was to be his last journey. A few days after his arrival in Laos he died quite unexpectedly.

Many people turned to Nakagawa Roshi for all sorts of reasons, and when there was no sesshin at the temple, a stream of visitors awaited him at all times. From my first week-long stay at Ryu-taku-ji I remember an elderly woman, nearly blind, who came to chant sutras in one of the shrines.

"She is a koto player, a teacher of the music of the koto instrument," said Roshi. "Now she is old, and it gets harder and harder for her. But always she has had faith and always she chants the sutras."

Two other visitors caught my eye during my first sojourn at the temple. A small frayed businessman turned up one evening with his large husky son, who was probably about nineteen years old. The son was dressed in a bright yellow turtleneck T-shirt and skintight dark green trousers. He carried a number of paperback books with lurid covers. His face was closed and sullen. After the evening chanting, the wan father was closeted for some time with the roshi. The sad little man left promptly after breakfast the next morning. His son remained at the temple, and he sat in the sun reading his books for several days; sometimes he did not even come to meals. On one of those days we all filed out of the dining area after lunch, following the roshi to the main hall for a special ceremony of sutra chanting. The sullen-faced young man was sprawled in the corridor in an ungraceful position. He was sound asleep. By his head was one of his many books, the cover of which was lively with undressed female figures. The roshi paused for a moment beside the sleeping form and spread a clean handkerchief on his head as protection against the sun, then with a gassho he stepped quietly over the sleeper and proceeded to his destination. We all followed him. The young man remained motionless.

When I returned to the temple for sesshin, this same individual, who had undoubtedly been deposited at the temple by a desperate parent, had not discarded his bright yellow turtleneck shirt, but the sullen look had left his face. In the early morning I saw him about the kitchen carrying pots and brooms. He did not sit in the meditation hall, but sometimes he propped himself on a barrel near the toilets, a sutra book in hand. He seemed to be intently concentrating, a surprising contrast to his languid perusal of the paperback books with lively covers. Possibly the sutra presents more of a challenge, I thought to myself.

The final morning of my Ryutaku-ji sesshin, I was almost too tired to sit in meditation in any acceptable position. My legs were swollen, and I could tell that I had a fever. When I returned to my room after the first ceremony of the day, I found beside my futon quilts a red lacquered box containing hard-boiled eggs, a piece of cheese, and some rice balls filled with a red bean paste. Next to the box was a small bottle of milk. These delicacies were accompanied by several fresh green leaves and a gossamer-thin paper napkin, all artistically arranged. Buddha's compassion! Roshi's old mother had brought this heartwarming gift to my room just after dawn. The food was a source of much-needed physical sustenance, but more important, my morale was sustained just as I had been on the verge of quitting the meditation hall altogether. Well, I thought, maybe I can get through at least another half-day.

I entered the roshi's sanzen room and made a rather tottery prostration. At the end of the dimly lit room, the roshi sat with his long wooden stick across his lap.

"Muuu . . ."

I seated myself cross-legged before him.

"Muuu . . ." intoned the roshi softly. "When you get lost in the dark countryside in a foreign country at night, Muuu; when your legs or head or something else ache in the zendo, Muuu; when a fly or an ant crawls on your face during zazen and you may not push it away, Muuu! Or maybe God. Muuu forever, no beginning, no end."

And the roshi rang his dismissal bell.

Intense awareness of everyone's final sesshin efforts filled the zendo; this tight atmosphere held the weary bodies upright even in our little segregated meditation room. We were watched over by a ferocious-faced wooden image of the temple's founder, Hakuin Zenji. On my return from one of the last required sanzen encounters I observed:

> Zenji's wooden nose—
> A painted hill the ant must
> Climb to Zenji's eyes.

Old Mrs. Nakagawa and the shaven-headed ex-pickpocket accompanied me by streetcar from Mishima to Numazu, where I was to catch a train for Kyoto. Conversation was limited to the extent of my not very adequate Japanese vocabulary. My companions wanted to ask many questions about America: "Larger mountains than in Japan?" "Many big cars and noisy trucks?" "Everybody very rich?" "No Buddhist temples in Massachusetts?" Mrs. Nakagawa found it difficult to comprehend that my husband, an only son, should live in America though his parents lived in Europe.

"And you have no children?" My dictionary was at the bottom of the suitcase, so for lack of vocabulary I replied, "No, I am very sorry but sickness makes this impossible." My companions shook their heads sympathetically. The reformed pickpocket said, "In Japan rich people like you adopt children."

"In Massachusetts, where we live," I said, "this is not permitted for Buddhists." My companions were astounded, and I was not able to explain properly the whys and wherefores of the matter.

Mrs. Nakagawa shook her head. "One cannot believe all that is written in the newspapers about foreign countries," she reflected.

"Different countries, different freedoms," observed the pickpocket sagely. "The people of Japan have wonderful karma," he continued. "We have the great teaching of Buddha. How fortunate we are, how very fortunate we are, aren't we!"

The train arrived at Numazu, and with my two companions I went to the roof cafeteria of a department store to await train time. The pickpocket went to buy orange juice and Mrs. Nakagawa went off to the camera department to pick up a pack of photographs. I sat at an outdoor table and watched some small children playing with balloons around a large fountain, under real branches with festoons of paper flowers wired onto them. It was a fine day. But it was quite a special day, as the day after a zazen retreat inevitably is. This mental bath, this mind-cleaning of sesshin, induces a sense of well-being that is infinitely more pleasing than even the physical well-being of a long hot bath. That day, after my first long sesshin, the world was miraculously new; everything, from the smallest speck of dust, the least prepossessing insect, to the warm sun and puffy clouds, had a strange clarity and appeared full of interest and importance.

The pickpocket appeared with three glasses of orange juice. As he sat down next to me his eye lit on my watch, a very small one, smaller than a ten-cent coin. He smiled and said like a child, shyly, "Oh beautiful, beautiful. Can I look at it?" I took it off and handed it to him. He turned it over and over in childlike wonder and absorption. "So very, very small and yet on it goes! Like flies' legs these watch hands, round and round and round, day after day." And he turned it over and around and studied it from every possible angle. Before returning it he held it in the palm of his deeply furrowed brown hand for a moment or two. There was a thoughtful, faraway look in his eyes. Then suddenly he smiled broadly, made a gassho, and returned it to me.

A few minutes later, Mrs. Nakagawa appeared with a yellow envelope of pictures. The roshi had asked her to show me these pictures before I left.

THE MAN WITH THE BAMBOO TRUNK 117

"Taken in the studio of his friend the artist." And she finally managed to convey that the artist in question was the one whose ink pictures the roshi had shown me in Cambridge, the artist who could not draw a smiling Christ.

The first photograph showed the artist seated in his studio with Nakagawa Roshi. Both wore ordinary black kimono of the sort sometimes worn by elderly shopkeepers. Both men had shaven heads. The artist had a beard, but there was nothing else to distinguish the Buddhist abbot from the Christian priest; they were just two Japanese men in a tatami-floored room surrounded by paper, brushes, and teacups.

Three of the photos fitted together to show a long and obviously large painting: a remarkable painting, possibly even a disturbing one to the orthodox Western Christian eye. Depicted rather in the style of a Maxfield Parrish storybook illustration was an extraordinary Resurrection scene. In the foreground were presumably Biblical characters: Moses, Daniel and his lions, Noah and his paired friends, as well as somber, bearded individuals who probably were meant to represent Old Testament worthies and prophets. I do not remember them very clearly. In the center foreground, the Virgin held a Christ child high above her head. The child's gaze was raised to the painting's central theme: a glowing, radiant Buddha figure surrounded by a nimbus of light. Faintly, in the background, could be seen the slightest suggestion of the form of a cross.

A curious thought passed through my mind. "Is it Buddha or Christ?" I asked Mrs. Nakagawa. She thought for a minute before replying.

"*Wakarimasen.* I don't know." Then after a little thought, she said, "Maybe both." Both, to be sure! Either-or is not a happy approach for a Japanese, who distrusts choices and cannot be at peace with himself until he has worked out a synthesis that excludes nothing and that completely embraces all.

Sesshin, the Zen retreat, is a beautiful and inspiring experience.

Nevertheless, it is arduous, and being a lesson in the endurance of the unendurable, it strains one's physical and mental capacities to the utmost. After the sesshin at Ryutaku-ji I retired to bed in a Kyoto hotel for three or four days. I was in a state of total exhaustion and had a very high fever. On about the second day of my indisposition there was a knock on my door. I made no reply, but the unlocked door was opened anyway to admit a small, middle-aged Japanese gentleman who bowed politely and placed his calling card on my bedside table, after which he launched into a long explanation in Japanese of who he was and what he wanted. My ears sang and I could not focus on either his face or his discourse. Somewhere in the middle of his speech I drifted back to sleep, and when I reawakened, or half-awakened, he was gone. Was he a dream, a hallucination? I wondered. But no, there was the calling card, with an unfamiliar name, a name I had never heard before. The mysterious stranger never tried to get in touch again, and as there was no telephone number on the card, I decided against pursuing the matter. Maybe there really was no *gaijin*, no foreigner, no me in the hotel bed. I could easily have been persuaded that she was almost anyone, or just as possibly no one, a no one possessing no preferences, no age, no nationality. The fever and the effects of mushin, self-naughting (as some Western writers like to translate this term), attempted in that temple at Mishima had set a thousand little fires inside my brain. Outside the partly open window could be heard the persistent plaint of automobile horns, the buzz of scooters, and the toc, toc, toc of wooden *geta* clogs on the sidewalks below. Toc, toc, toc, an eternal hustling from somewhere to nowhere: relentless, unswerving, quixotic pursuit!

8 THE ORPHAN

Sin and evil
are not to be got rid of
just blindly;
look at the astringent persimmons!
They turn into the sweet dried ones.

ABOUT TEN DAYS LATER, I felt myself again. I set out for Nagoya with the professor of Sanskrit from Kyushu University whom I had tutored in English and who had kindly urged me to visit his country some years before. Professor Ihara and I had accepted an invitation to visit a Zen temple in Nagoya, the Myoko-ji.

Sokan Kawano, abbot of Myoko-ji, was a small, vigorous man with piercing eyes, "like a snake's," as he put it cheerfully. He was particularly concerned with the welfare of orphans. This interest was easy to understand, as he was an orphan himself, his adoptive father having been the former abbot of Myoko-ji, a Zen master who had died at the age of 104.

Our host had spent eight years as the master of a temple in Mukden. He had arrived there during the Japanese occupation of that Manchurian city. While the city was briefly under Russian control, the Japanese population was evacuated or imprisoned. This energetic little priest was among the few Japanese not molested by the Russian authorities. The Japanese flag was lowered in the temple courtyard and the Russian flag raised in its place. The abbot's patrons were no longer able to give alms for the children's food, and furthermore, a more heart-breaking situation had developed in the wake of the closing down of the Japanese colony. The Russian authorities had decided that Japanese residents could return to their own country, but only if they were old enough to walk out of their homes by themselves. All babies not old enough to walk were to be left in their homes along with furniture and other possessions. This decree, possibly unofficial, was enforced by bayonet-carrying soldiers, who, after forcing the distraught mothers of young children from their homes to waiting buses, proceeded to board up the abandoned houses, leaving the tiny occupants to a dreadful fate. We asked the abbot how he was able to rescue some of these luckless infants.

"Well," he replied, "I had always to wait until after dark. Then quietly, taking care to avoid military police, I wandered through the dark streets, listening always for the sound of a whimper or a cry. Sometimes the sound was faint and I had to listen very carefully. Getting into the houses was also a problem and it was necessary to be very careful and quiet. As the days went by, the cries became fainter, and my ears almost came off my head with my efforts to listen. Always I had to be extremely careful not to attract attention. Then came the typhoid and other sicknesses; nearly everyone was ill and many of the children died. I did not dare remain in bed; always I thought there will be somewhere another child waiting. I grew thin and some people round about named me Old Snake Eyes. I caught the fever and sometimes I wondered if I could get out of bed, then through my brain, maybe through my heart, another whimper and I would think to myself just one more, just one more time. I will try just once again."

"That is the real Bodhisattva's way," said Professor Ihara. "That is the Great Compassion."

"Compassion," said the abbot thoughtfully. "So often one hears this word, so often this compassion is talked about. And what does it really mean? one may well ask. Compassion, as it actually works out, is simply endurance. Without patient endurance, maybe true compassion is almost impossible. Yes, it is necessary to endure, just once more, just one more time. People inquire, 'Why should anyone want to spend all day sitting in zazen?' and I tell them that zazen is endurance. It is important to realize the necessity for endurance."

The abbot walked with us around the rather extensive grounds surrounding his large temple. A recent typhoon had uprooted many enormous trees, and we admired the way they had all carefully been propped; some even had cracked branches tied up in a sort of splint. The abbot stopped here and there to inspect a patient. "Trees, like children, have their own place. They are important to us and we are important to them. A Buddhist knows that the birds, the trees, the earth itself should be treated with as much care as human children. Nothing should be neglected."

Professor Ihara inquired about the orphanages in which the abbot was supposed to have a particular interest.

"Orphanages, yes, there are many orphanages in this prefecture. Nevertheless, I always think the largest and most important orphanage in the world is Buddhism and one need not go about looking for some special place, some special institution. All things should be taken care of like orphans; if a few people can really learn this, then Zen training means something."

An American disciple living in the temple told us: "This abbot, I really have confidence in him. He is a good man. Sometimes he bears down on us with fire in his eye, and he can be quite ferocious, even in some things intransigent. But there is always a good reason. I've met quite a few Zen monks since I came to Japan. Some are good, of course. But I have learned a lot, seen a lot here. I used to be very idealistic; American Buddhists usually are. I have found that there are very few monks like our abbot. I have even met one or two who are real demons right out of hell, sadistic, aggressive, and unbelievably arrogant. Once I complained to the abbot. He only shook his head sadly and talked about 'dreadful karma.' He doesn't criticize people much and he doesn't pay a lot of attention to others' criticism. The young monks criticize each other quite a bit. They are modern and they complain, for example, when the abbot insists that so many of us spend a lot of time picking up every bottle, paper cup, and candy wrapper left by schoolchildren and trippers. A great many children and tourists come here, whole busloads in fact. The place looks like a public dump after they have left and we novices must go out and clean everything up, we must not leave a single gum paper. Some of the temple masters' sons don't like that. They would rather be back in their college libraries reading about Buddhism, arguing about the significance of some Sanskrit words. But Roshi, the abbot, that is, tells them that their theories of philosophy are as much real Buddhism as a rice bowl full of Sanskrit words is a meal of rice.

"Americans often have a rather distorted idea of what life in a Zen temple is like," the young American continued. "In California people who are interested in Buddhism talk endlessly about enlightenment. Lots of people talk about enlightenment; even those who are not interested in Buddhism think they are interested in something called 'Zen enlightenment.' Here we just get up in the morning, go about our business paying close attention to everything we do, or trying to. Things have to be done carefully. We do zazen, go to sanzen, and one season follows another in the usual way."

"But there are teachers in Japan who talk about enlightenment or write about it," I observed.

"Well, in America there are Bible-thumpers who talk as though they've just been on a guided tour through Heaven. But from another point of view, some of the people who think it's chic and intellectual to talk about enlightenment would tell you you were superstitious if you started to talk about a Christian Heaven. Rather curious, if you start to think about it. Or actually, maybe it isn't. But what is big in Japanese Buddhism is the common-sense thing. Japanese Buddhism is many things, of course, but the common-sense, the down-to-earth thing that you get into deeper and deeper through Zen practice, Westerners I knew in California never talked about at all.

"And, you know, in our country there is this big hang-up about the importance of people and the unimportance of things. You make a big point about how important people are to you and how unimportant things are in your life. It's *in* to say, 'I like people, not things!' Here one learns that people and things cannot be separated, and that when even things are treated with care and respect, people are not treated as things."

One day, a luncheon party was planned. The abbot, several of his monks including the young American, Professor Ihara, and I walked about a mile to a nearby town to catch a bus. We stood about talking at the corner of a narrow street lined with small musty shops. Suddenly from somewhere, a child started to cry. The abbot's expression was impassive for a minute or two, but when the crying increased a look of pain crossed his face. Then he was off down the road, his wooden clogs leaving deep impressions in the wet black mud. A block or so away, a plump toddler of about three wailed his distress as he seemed to be in the process of relieving himself through his cotton jumper and down his legs.

"There he goes again, our abbot," said one of the monks rather sheepishly. "It is a kind of complex with him, he just cannot hear a baby cry! The reason does not matter to him; you know, there is always something with babies. They are wet, they are tired, they break a toy, or maybe they just wish to make a lot of noise. Still, the abbot cannot hear that crying without going to look."

"One of the senior monks who traveled with him overnight on a sleeper train told me this story," said the American. "It was a hot night and somewhere at the end of the car a baby cried. After a few minutes, the monk heard a dreadful banging and thumping on the berth above him, so he climbed up and looked between the curtains. The abbot was having a nightmare. It seemed he was trying to break through the wall of the train, and he was so obsessed with his efforts that it was hard to wake him up and to persuade him that he was on a train and trying to break right through it. He made a lot of noise, the abbot did, and faces appeared from sleeping berths around as people wanted to see where the disturbance was coming from."

As the American finished speaking, the abbot emerged from behind a car beside a small fat housewife with frizzy hair. The housewife had wrapped her child in a towel and was pulling him after her by the hand. The abbot was trying to placate the screaming infant. Finally he held out a large bright orange and the screams stopped. The child was given the orange and the abbot returned to his waiting company, apparently soothed. But on a closer look, his face was flushed. The "snake eyes" were clouded with sadness.

Bonno soku bodai, "suffering is also enlightenment," it says in one of the sutras. A glowing Sun-faced Buddha is also the Bodhisattva who is one with the sufferer, one with suffering itself.

9 IN THE BLUE DRAGON'S CAVE

*On the lotus leaf
the dew of this world
is distorted.*

Issa

According to the Zen classic the *Hekigan Roku,* or "Blue Cliff Records," those in search of truth must descend not once but many times into the depths of the "blue dragon's cave." There is a Chinese legend that jewels of great price lie hidden in the throat of an enormous blue dragon. This legend was adopted by Zen teachers, who used it to symbolize the necessity for long and arduous experience in the darkest regions of the psyche.

I thrashed about in these turbid realms whenever the symptoms of a chronic and painful disease manifested themselves. This problem had plagued me on and off since adolescence. Medicines and operations failed to put my anatomy in order and could not rescue me from the labyrinth dwelling of the horrid blue dragon. Some people I knew talked a great deal about peace of mind. They admired the heroic austerities of different religions or pseudoreligious practices. Is Buddhism simply a matter of asceticism? I wondered. Is equanimity proof of a Buddhist spirit, and if one has strong nerves, the capacity for self-discipline, and detachment, does one "prove" one's religion? Is true religion in need of justification? Or is the need for justification simply an egotistic preoccupation with the individual and collective image? An exaggerated preoccupation with apologetics, I decided, could develop into a source of delusion. Furthermore, I reflected, quests for ecstasy and certainty, whether aided by austerities or by drugs, might result in *prajna* (wisdom) intuition, but only if it were not forgotten that consciousness is in a constant state of becoming. A curious experience that I had once while hospitalized for surgery was the source of one or two valuable insights.

Late one night I was given an injection, probably a tranquilizer or painkiller. I decided that the effect was inadequate, that I just could not cope with any further physical or psychic unpleasantness. It seemed to me that the doctor's efforts could be assisted with some of my own codeine pills, which I had brought with me in a stationery box. In a rather hazy frame of mind, I swallowed two or three, or maybe more. After an initial period of dizziness, nausea, and cloudy ruminations, the room suddenly grew alarmingly dim. Then gradually the darkness began to dissipate, and after a little time I found myself enveloped in a sweet-smelling bluish mist. As the mist closed in, I seemed to become weightless and finally melted peacefully into a softly undulating blue and silver blanket of clouds. Flowers appeared in wild profusion, and some of the clouds parted to reveal myriad glistening prisms of light and color. From somewhere beyond the clouds there arose and swelled a sublime monotonal sound; was it that all-embracing bell of St. Briac? I wondered. But no, it was not a bell I had ever heard before. Perhaps it was not a bell at all but the voice of the prism. I was transformed into shimmering luminous waves that rose and ebbed in a sphere where sound, color, and smell were indistinguishable, where all was timelessly wonderful and joyful. However, the most important aspect of the experience was not its sensuous qualities but rather an accompanying awareness that all humanity, all beings, all creation belong together in a way that was mysteriously and incomprehensibly veiled by my colorful visions. The visions, the delusions, whatever they were, were not at the heart of the matter. Only the intuition of the unity of myself with all creation was deep and enduring.

It did not last long, that marvelous state. Suddenly, far more suddenly than it had appeared, it began to fade. This sublime condition was replaced by a brief vision of distant spires and turrets. Then that vision, too, completely vanished. For a few minutes I longed for a return to the sphere of blessedness, for a continuation of the enchanted realm of visions. I must describe it, write it all down, I thought. I fished through my belongings in the drawer of the bedside table, where a large pad of lined paper could be found but no pencil. I used a small hard lipstick instead, and I wrote for what seemed like hours. At last I fell asleep in the middle of a sentence. The next morning I awakened early, before the nurse came in. The lipstick was still in my hand; I had written nearly forty pages. But, alas, the words were meaningless or indistinguishable. The pad was full of undecipherable words and slurred scribbles that were not words at all; at least I could not read them.

Well, it was gone. I felt rested and comforted; a languorous equanimity prevailed. There was no immediate need to return to the beautiful and mysterious realm. In fact, I have not been there since, though I often thought about the experience with the advent, some years later, of psychedelic "trips" and the possibly misguided cult of inner explorations. I have never felt a desire for psychedelic adventures.

My experience brings to mind one of the parables of the Lotus Sutra, the parable of the magic city. A party of friends set out in search of a fabled treasure city, where they believed they could live forever in comfort, peace, and happiness. The road was long and hard. Finally, many members of the party became exhausted and discouraged, so they decided to turn back. Their leader, however, felt compassion for them, and by means of some sort of magic, he conjured up a mirage, a city wherein all the exhausted searchers were able to find rest and much-needed encouragement. When all were recovered and heartened, the leader caused the illusion or hallucination to vanish, after which he said to his friends: "We must be on our way again, and in time we will reach our destination. Now you are rested and refreshed, and you are better able to endure the difficulties and hardships that we all must face before we arrive at our true destination. We must continue on until we finally reach our true home, the place where our destiny is to be fulfilled."

"Have you ever visited the famous Mount Auburn Cemetery?" nearly all of my Japanese friends used to inquire of their English tutor. "It is beautiful in spring, the most beautiful spot in Cambridge, when the fruit trees and magnolias are in blossom!" As it happens, many of my ancestors, including the two ladies quoted earlier in this book, were planted in this remarkable park with its stately trees, its ponds and hills, extraordinary statuary, and curious Gothic chapels. I was always obliged to admit that I had never seen that particular cemetery in the spring, since the people in my family whose funerals I had attended there had died during the cold months of the year, when all was appropriately brown and bleak. However, I had seen, as had few of my Japanese pupils, the ancient cemetery on Japan's Mount Koya with its eleven-hundred-year-old Hall of Ten Thousand Lights and its enormous trees, where mist and pine-scented incense drifted over and around the moss-covered stone lanterns.

The burial grounds of Cambridge and of Mount Koya, one of

the centers of the esoteric Buddhist disciplines called *mikkyo* in Japanese, fused in the karma of an interesting Bostonian named William Sturgis Bigelow. He must have been the first New Englander, indeed one of the first Americans, to enter the blue dragon's cave in search of Buddhist treasure. Dr. Sturgis Bigelow was the grandson of the physician-founder of the Mount Auburn burial park, and half of his ashes are buried there. The other half of his ashes are buried in Japan. He was probably the first American to devote more than thirty years to the esoteric Buddhist meditation practices and disciplines of the Tendai-Shingon tradition, one of whose historic centers was established by the great Kobo Daishi on Mount Koya over a thousand years ago.

In the past decade, considerable interest has developed in this subtle and complicated method for conveying Buddhist insights and intuitions. Refugee Tibetan teachers have settled in India, Europe, and the United States. Most Tibetan monks belong to the school of Buddhism represented in Japan by the monks of Mount Koya. However, one wonders how many of today's young Westerners who avidly peruse the ever-growing number of paperback books on mandalas and esoteric practices will ever devote themselves to years of intense practice as did Dr. Bigelow in his lifelong quest. Some of the more unfortunate drug trips organized by psychologist gurus have led into the dragon's cave, into regions that Dr. Bigelow explored without drugs, first in Japan with a teacher and later in Boston without help or guidance, in his search for enlightenment.

Dr. Bigelow was the scion of a distinguished Boston family. A man of a complex personality, in his youth he was known to many of his contemporaries as a dandy and a writer of witty and frivolous letters, who admired and courted a famous opera singer and who gave elegant dinners to the fashionable and politically eminent. President Theodore Roosevelt often stayed in the doctor's Beacon Street house when visiting Boston. Dr. Bigelow's collection of Japanese art, now in the Boston Museum of Fine

Arts, was a labor of discrimination as well as of dedication. It is the largest and finest such collection in the world outside Tokyo.

Yet there was another Dr. Bigelow whom friends and relatives seldom, if ever, encountered. Even lifelong friends rarely caught glimpses of a persona whose existence was guarded in the shadow of privacy. Social and psychic survival in a Calvinist climate demands an outward appearance of self-confidence in the midst of bustling, frenetic activity. Originally these were taken as outward signs that one was on the way to salvation. But when belief in otherworldly salvation gave place to belief in society, the façade of confidence and bustle finally deteriorated into criteria for social acceptance in the mercantile society these Calvinists had created. Self-doubts or a dearth of concrete results in one's chosen profession or career are painful afflictions for the Calvinist conscience. Sturgis Bigelow, the son and grandson of two distinguished physicians, studied medicine in Boston, Paris, and Vienna. However, his two years of medical practice brought him no satisfaction, either emotional or intellectual, in the career that had brought eminence and wealth to both his father and grandfather. In 1880 he left Boston for Japan with his friend the art critic Ernest Fenollosa. There, through his interest in Japanese art and culture, he learned about the practices of mikkyo. For some years he seems to have entertained an optimistic belief that only time and application were needed to achieve concrete results and to find rational answers to his metaphysical questions about the meaning of life and about the nature of mind and matter. The doctor's nineteenth-century rationalism demanded concrete results and literal answers. The relationship of mind and body, of body and consciousness, especially preoccupied him.

After seven years in Japan he returned to Boston, where he continued his daily practice of mikkyo, even after the death of his teacher. However, as he grew older and his health, never robust, began to deteriorate, he began to despair of ever emerging from the dragon's cave.

The answers to the questions that had first inspired his spiritual search were not forthcoming. In 1902 he made another journey to Japan for further instruction from his teacher's successor. His meditation practice continued and deepened to the point where the delusions created by his exercises in concentration could hardly be separated from physical reality. Finally, in 1915, he was in great distress, both physical and spiritual. There seemed to be no escape from the cave, and the treasure was hidden in the black recesses far beyond his view.

One of the closest friends of his later years, with whom a warm correspondence developed, was a Roman Catholic convert, Margaret Chanler. Mrs. Chanler was blessed with urbanity, a warm heart, and an engaging lack of missionary zeal unusual in an American Catholic of her era. She was interested in the doctor's Buddhist meditations and speculations; he, in turn, learned something about the mystical side of Catholicism from his Catholic correspondent. The lady addressed her Buddhist friend as "Dearest Hierophant" because she saw him as a "revealer of mysteries."

Of her "Hierophant" she wrote in her memoirs: "He had a distinguished personality, . . . a little aloof . . . he was full of Buddhist lore and emanated a peaceful radiance mingled with a faint suggestion of toilet water. . . . He was infinitely kind and generous, much beloved by his friends—not only for the gifts, rare and precious as they often were, with which he punctuated the course of a friendship, but because of the stimulating something there was about his mind and conversation, because he made things happen, and perhaps because he was not happy himself, but tried to bring happiness about for others."*

Of their discussions of the life of the spirit, and of Dr. Bigelow's interpretation of Buddhism, Margaret Chanler wrote: "Buddhism, as Dr. Bigelow understood it, seems to seek salvation in

*This and the quotations in the following two paragraphs are from Margaret Chanler's *Autumn in the Valley* (Boston, Little, Brown & Co., 1936).

nothingness and to attain holiness without love. But it must not be forgotten that the early Catholic missionaries to the Far East allowed their converts from Buddhism to venerate Gautama Buddha as a saint, so deeply edifying was all his life and teaching, so consonant with what they themselves believed. The two religions hold much in common; but Christianity begins and ends with God, and Love is the essence of its being. On this Dr. Bigelow and I could never agree; he knew a great deal about what seemed to me the almost mechanical relation of the soul to the body and the spiritual acrobatics it could perform, but Divinity was an empty word to him and I could not do without it. Our friendship prospered in spite of this fundamental antinomy, and our discussions left each of us exhilarated with a sense of having been right."

Of Dr. Bigelow's spiritual distress and isolation, Mrs. Chanler observed: "It must be hard to take comfort in a creed totally alien to one's race and tradition, with no one near who shares the same faith. St. John of the Cross says somewhere—I quote from memory—that a burning coal placed on a marble floor will inevitably char and grow cold."

Had Sturgis Bigelow lived in another age, another place, he might have entered a monastic community and benefited from the encouragement and support of fellow seekers. But his world was New England, a New England dominated by an uncompromising dogma that condemned everyone to compulsive busyness, preferably in the marketplace, or failing that, in the drawing room. The Catholic mystics of the Middle Ages well knew the "dark night of the soul," as they called it, the "cloud of unknowing." They were wise enough to realize that "energetics," however benevolent, and enlightenment are not necessarily related. However, possibly Sturgis Bigelow's lonely search had one great advantage. He never became distracted by the delusions created by the security and consolation of a collective ego, by compulsive togetherness. Exclusivism, bigotry, and intolerance find a fertile soil in many religious communities where intense asceticism, an anti-intellectual bias, and a vigorous esprit de corps are too assiduously cultivated.

The correspondence of Sturgis Bigelow with one of his Buddhist mentors is kept in the Tendai Buddhist temple of Homyo-in in Otsu, Japan. Memorial services were held for the doctor in this temple after his death, and half of his ashes are buried here, beside the ashes of his friend Ernest Fenollosa. Dr. Bigelow's correspondence of 1890 to 1921 with the temple master is carefully preserved in the temple archives. In these letters, expressed with honesty and courtesy, are queries, doubts, misgivings, and despondencies. Like many of today's young people, Dr. Bigelow was attracted by what one writer calls the "instrumentality" of Buddhist meditation disciplines. He followed the instructions given him in Japan with great care and devotion. However, as the years passed, honest scrutiny of himself did not reveal the results, the superior strength of character and selflessness he sought. One of the last of the series of letters written to the master of Homyo-in* came from the depths of the dragon's cave:

10 June, 1921

. . . I hope your health is good. Mine is not good either spiritually or physically. . . . At present I can hardly walk across the room even with a cane. Spiritually my condition is still worse. *This is entirely my own fault.* It is said in the Kyo [sutra] that folly, lust and anger are three of the principle sources of trouble with everybody. In myself the last seems less important than the first two. Certainly everything has been done to help me that possibly could be done. I am most unworthy of it but my appreciation and gratitude are beyond the power of words to express. When a bronze founder casts

*Quoted in "Selected Letters of William Sturgis Bigelow," edited by Akiko Murakata (unpublished doctoral dissertation, George Washington University), with the permission of Homyo-in, Otsu, Shiga Prefecture, Japan.

a statue of Buddha there are sometimes flaws in the work. When these are not too large the defective part is cut out and sound metal put in its place. When the defects are very large, the statue must be melted over again and cast afresh. But if the metal itself is bad nothing can help. The statue will be full of defects no matter how many times it is cast. So with human beings also. It is easier to make bronze Buddhas than real ones. Bonnos [delusions and sins] may be cut out. But if the metal itself is soft and weak then there is nothing to be done. It is not possible to make a rope of sea sand or to make a wet towel stand on end no matter how long one tries. And there is no place in the universe for wet towels. Therefore I hope and pray for obliteration, not of my bonnos but of myself. All religions, so far as I know, are founded on the wish for a continuation of existence. This thing called existence is said to be happy or unhappy according to the previous conduct of the individual, but what I want is *the complete stoppage of all existence of any kind in any world.* I know I think what you will say, you will remind me of the hotsugan [the vow to attain Buddhahood despite all obstacles] and especially of the words: "shujo muhen seigan do" [sentient beings are infinite; vow to save them all]. It is a very solemn and a beautiful oath, but I am unable to keep it. As well might an eel make an oath to stand on the end of his tail. I want neither heaven nor hell nor anything between. All I want is obliteration that is the cessation of existence.

I said this to a member of my own family who has been much attached to me since early childhood. She said very sweetly, "What kind of a heaven do you suppose I shall have without you?" To which I answered, "It will appear to you that I am there but I shall not be full of defects as I am here but exactly as you want me to be and as you believe that I am, irrespective of what I really am." Some other person might also want me in their heaven but for different qualities. It is obvious that I cannot be in both at once, therefore it is clear that I must seem to be what they wish me to be. For you or me this is easy to understand. But for those young people this is very difficult. They say, "then heaven is imaginary." To which I answer, "It certainly is and so also is the present world."

As this may be the last opportunity I shall have of writing to you I want to thank you most cordially and sincerely for all your kindness to me. In 1886, on the first day of the fifth month . . . I asked you what the fundamental idea of Buddhism was. You answered, "kindness and help to others." Since then you have shown me much kindness and given me much help. . . . You answered many questions, and the last time I came to the temple you gave me many precious things so that I was almost afraid to admire anything for fear you would give it to me. . . .

Since Mr. Okakura's death there is no one in this country to whom I can talk of Buddhism. The Yasokyo [Christianity] is divided into two churches, one of which, Romakyo [Roman Catholicism], uses mikkyo, but the other of which does not teach mikkyo at all. I do not think they even know what it is. The Romakyo is active and powerful but appears to be principally occupied with the things of this world and in affirming and solidifying its own existence. I think perhaps their samaji [meditation] does not go beyond the first stage and the Buddhist idea of imparting merit accumulated by the Bosatsu equally to all mankind appears to be unknown to them. . . .

With this I bid you a respectful and grateful farewell. I am dying physically by slow degrees without pain. I should be glad to commit seppuku [suicide] only, of course, a physical seppuku is inadequate and does not interrupt the action of Innen [karma, cause and effect]. What I want is a spiritual seppuku that will finish me once for all. But unfortunately I am so ignorant that I do not know how to do it. Can you tell me of any kind friend who will act as my assistant and cut my spiritual head off when I get through with my physical body?

Respectfully yours,
Gesshin

Dr. Bigelow died in 1926, five years after the above letter was written. A contemporary has written of the peace and serenity that he seemed to have found shortly before his death. "The greater the doubt, the greater the enlightenment" goes an old Zen saying. It is probable that Dr. Bigelow did indeed overcome his preoccupation with the mechanics of spirituality, with self-improvement, and experienced the Truth in which Thoreau found that "solitude is not solitude . . . nor weakness weakness," the "peace which passeth all understanding."

Dr. Bigelow once told his Buddhist teacher that he thought both teachers and pupils would be spared a lot of unnecessary effort if the student of mikkyo could be told the "object" of this traditional discipline. Unfortunately, as Dr. Bigelow discovered for himself, this is just what cannot be taught: each person must learn for himself, from his own experience in the dragon's cave, what the object is *not*.

Nearly half a century has passed since Dr. Bigelow's death. During that time a vast number of Americans have discovered that affluence, preoccupation with communality, and social activism, though bringing many material and other beneficent innovations, are not adequate for the realization of the spiritual quest. "Be up and be doing . . . activity activity . . . this will be most likely to be followed and rewarded by Triumphant Satisfactions," wrote the redoubtable Cotton Mather. However, no accomplishment, no matter how great a triumph, brings peace to the neo-Calvinist heart. The great need of the latter-day disciples of Cotton Mather is for activity, usefulness, service. Their own. It is more blessed to give than to receive, and the New England Calvinist and his descendants have never for a moment doubted the value of what they wished to give to the world. Or have they? Could all their self-important hustle and bustle conceal a few nagging doubts?

10 A ZEN CATHOLIC ROSHI

Rain, hail and snow,
ice, too, are set apart,
but when they fall—
the same water
of the valley stream.

THANKS TO THE WIDELY READ BOOKS of such writers as Daisetz T. Suzuki, Nancy Wilson Ross, Alan Watts, Christmas Humphreys, and Huston Smith, the 1960s was a period when many hundreds of people, particularly in artistic and intellectual circles, were inspired to investigate Buddhist spirituality. There were also individuals who found their inspiration indirectly, in the writings of Aldous Huxley, Erich Fromm, T. S. Eliot, or Joseph Campbell. During these same years, two large Buddhist institutions were established in California and New York: the San Francisco Zen Center and the New York Zen Studies Society. These centers grew with surprising rapidity; by 1971 the San Francisco Zen Center had become one of the largest centers for Zen meditation in the world, and the Zen Studies Society was only slightly smaller. Furthermore, the number of small groups formed for the practice of Buddhist zazen was considerable. In Cambridge, Massachusetts, the Venerable Chimyo Horioka, a Japanese priest of the Shingon school, has given instruction in zazen for more than fifteen years.

Every year an enormous number of people have entered and will continue to enter the dragon's cave as they become involved in Buddhist meditation practices. Some are experimenting with cults of religious excitement, Buddhist and otherwise, that promise superior psychic techniques for growth. The process of searching out saints and supermen to oversee their progress opens a new chapter in the interesting history of American religion.

In September, 1963, a Buddhist retreat for Westerners was held in a private house on Cape Cod, Massachusetts. The retreat was planned to last three days, and many preparations were necessary. Arrangements had to be worked out carefully so that the retreat could be carried on in the traditional silence; food, beds, and other necessities had to be prepared for about seventeen participants.

It was a humid Indian summer day. Pheasant calls and the voices of mourning doves were blown off the sand dunes behind my mother's summer cottage, where I sat on the flagstone terrace cutting up vegetables for an enormous casserole. I thought about the old Japanese teacher who was to be in charge of the retreat. He was a popular roshi who had led an ordinary family life: he was a father and many times a grandfather, and there were also great-grandchildren. His singleminded, intense practice and natural austerity were impressive. Lay people in particular, both Japanese and American, were greatly drawn to his cult of excitement, to his promises of *kensho*—a kind of conversion, a glimpse of the Void—for all who applied themselves with vigor and wholeheartedness.

The experiences that various people sustained under his tutelage were much discussed in certain quarters. Unquestionably, most of these experiences were valuable and the emotions they evoked in his pupils genuine enough. In the old monk's small temple in Japan kenshos were cultivated; the experience of the oneness of self and cosmos was excitedly sought through long hours of zazen in an atmosphere of hysterical expectation overseen by shouting, *kyosaku*-wielding monitors. We did not wish for and were not expecting this modus operandi for our Cape Cod retreat, despite its great popularity both in Japan and in our own country. It appealed to intellectuals, artists, and businessmen. People too sophisticated for a Christian revivalist service eagerly sought spiritual rebirth and peace of mind in a kensho awakening. Possibly the old roshi would have agreed with the nineteenth-century American divine who justified the religious revivals, the "Great Awakenings," that swept the east coast of the United States in the middle of the nineteenth century in the following manner: "As yet the state of the . . . world is such, that to expect to promote religion without excitement is unphilosophical and absurd. The great political and other-worldly excitements that agitate Christendom are all unfriendly to religion, and divert the mind from the interests of the soul. Now these excitements can only be counteracted by *religious excitements*. And until there is religious principle in the world to put down irreligious excitements, it is vain to promote religion, except by countering excitements. This is . . . a historical fact."*

The Reverend Charles Finney rejected all metaphysical speculation and maintained that "experience is all . . . it is a matter of consciousness." How eagerly we Americans seek intense experience and how quick we are to identify intensity of emotion with truth! Or we swing to the opposite extreme and cultivate a sterile, pretentious, but equally emotional "objectivity," which, we foolishly persuade ourselves, is far above all emotions, our own and other people's.

*Charles Grandison Finney, quoted in Perry Miller, *The Life of the Mind in America: From the Revolution to the Civil War* (New York, Harcourt, Brace & World, 1965).

My reverie was interrupted by the sound of an approaching automobile in the long, narrow dirt avenue. The roshi and his interpreters were expected from New York. They were being driven to Cape Cod by a Viennese lady psychiatrist, whom we affectionately called our Frau Doctor. "She doesn't look like a psychiatrist," people often said of her. Indeed, with her elegantly arranged white hair and delicate features, she should have spent her days surrounded by silks and satins and by strains of Mozart instead of in an austere doctor's office clad in tweeds and twills. However, her eighteenth-century femininity was complemented by a twentieth-century vigor and forthrightness.

As she emerged from the car (the roshi and his assistant had been delivered to their destination, a house nearby, several minutes earlier) with sweaters, blankets, and picnic baskets under each arm, she exclaimed: "Well, we are late. But there is a good reason. We have had such an interesting time this afternoon! On the way here it occurred to me that the roshi should see Narragansett Bay, and then it seemed like a wonderful opportunity for him to visit an American Christian monastery. When we arrived in Providence, I telephoned to the Catholic monastery on the coast, which is presided over by the author of that book called *Zen Catholicism*.* The prior invited us all for tea. After our arrival, first we were shown about the beautiful church and gardens, and then the prior gave us tea. The roshi and the prior had an opportunity for some discussion. I think it was enormously worthwhile."

"I don't suppose all Catholic priests are as hostile to non-Catholics as the Irish clergy or the clergy of Vietnam," I said. "How did those Catholic monks receive the roshi?"

"Oh well," said Frau Doctor, "at first there was quite a bit of 'who are you anyway?' sort of atmosphere, but as soon as the roshi and the prior sat down together and got to talking that

*Dom Aelred Graham, *Zen Catholicism* (New York, Harcourt, Brace & World, 1963).

phase passed quickly. Some of the younger monks had a good look at the Buddhist monastic clothes, which they had obviously not seen before, but the reception was remarkably friendly. It was spontaneous, it was really a fine thing."

"What did they discuss?" I inquired.

"The prior—he is English, you know—asked the roshi why Buddhist monks are burning themselves in Vietnam. He listened attentively while the roshi explained to him that a Buddhist monk would only kill himself, burn himself, that is, as a last resort and in order to focus attention on a really desperate problem for which no other solution would seem possible. The prior seemed to understand and to appreciate the roshi's answer. I am glad we had this experience. It was good for a few Catholics and Buddhists to have tea together and to discuss the nasty business between their religions that is going on in Vietnam and is all over the front pages of our newspapers. That prior seemed really interested in Buddhism, much more than one would imagine from reading his book *Zen Catholicism*. He has practiced some sort of zazen himself. But of course we have to remember that Catholics cannot sit down and write just anything they think or exactly as they might wish. There's always an official handout and their censors to be kept in mind. Face to face the prior is open-hearted and responsive. Really an open mind. We told him that we were on our way to a Zen Buddhist retreat on Cape Cod with the roshi. The prior was greatly interested. He said that Catholic contemplatives should learn how to do zazen and that he would like to take part in one of our retreats himself sometime."

"Well," I said, "it is hard to imagine that possibility, but what a good thing it would be if human lions and lambs, so to speak, could actually lie down, or, in this case, I should say sit down together in peace. Possibly a lot could be learned from such an endeavor." This was in the days when I was mistakenly persuaded that most Catholics were ferocious (in all pertaining to their religion) and nearly all Buddhists devoted to tolerance and pacifism. As for the author of *Zen Catholicism,* this was the second time I had heard about him.

The first time I had heard of this venerable Catholic prior was one snowy afternoon early in the spring of that same year. A Japanese friend who was a resident of Harvard University's comparative religion department—sometimes known as God's Motel because its modern building is designed like a motel, with living accommodations for students of comparative religion—had arrived for a visit, bringing with him *Zen Catholicism,* a captivating title.

My Japanese friend had found the possibilities for learning about "religion as it is actually practiced and taught in the Western world" rather limited at Harvard.

"The professor pulls down a big map and with a long stick he points to England. Then we have some descriptions of what he saw and thought about while he was a missionary in Southeast Asia. . . . However, that is just not what I want to learn while I am in this interesting country of yours, where all kinds of remarkable and unusual religions are to be found." So my friend bought a bicycle. He cycled to every church and religious institution for miles around and collected an amazing assortment of religious literature and artifacts. He acquired a special identification card that permitted him to attend Black Muslim services: "very sincere and ardent," he found them.

"Look here," said Shimpu (this nickname, meaning "priest," was acquired because of the number of letters he received addressing him as "Father"). "I have found at least three sects who know every nook and corner of the Christian heavens and hells, and even exactly how many people are going to get in there, as well as what they want to do with everybody else! And what about this? Last week I found some people in Boston who pass out specially blessed handkerchiefs. You are supposed to make a wish and then put the handkerchief under your pillow."

"Have you tried one out?" I asked.

"Of course," he replied, "and that kind of blessing doesn't work, at least it doesn't work for me!"

Shimpu's career at Harvard was no doubt unique. He discovered in one of the many religious newspapers to which he subscribed an advertisement for a movie called *The Idolatrous Practices and Heathen Beliefs of the Unconverted Minions of Darkness in Japan,* or something to that effect. The movie could be borrowed free by religious groups or institutions.

"Of course they would be pleased to send it to Harvard," said Shimpu and ordered it forthwith, prefixing his name with "The Reverend." He was quite qualified to do this, as he had received ordination from one of the ancient centers of Buddhism in Japan.

A night was chosen for the showing, to which were invited a few Hindus, a scholar from a Moslem country, and about half a dozen divinity students, presumably studying to become Christian ministers. The movie was in color and showed historic Japanese temples, shrines, and colorful processions, while in the background a lugubrious voice pointed out the infamies and described the unredeemed nature of non-Christian beliefs in that country. When the movie was finished, and before anyone could get out of his or her seat, Shimpu quickly passed out large sheets of paper and pencils and asked his guests to describe their impressions of the show. "Then," he said, "when you have given me your thoughts, we shall have tea and Japanese cake." Unfortunately, none of his Christian guests was in the mood for exposition, and they squirmed out of their chairs and left. Not very sporting of them, I thought, but at least one did have the grace to remark as he left: "That is not Christianity. Real Christians do not make and send around movies like that."

Shimpu made quite regular visits to a Catholic chapel in downtown Boston. "I go there for two reasons," he told me. "First, I am collecting a series of pamphlets by a father whose name is Bumble, or possibly it's Rumble, who is an Australian and who writes about every sect of Christianity, describing them in such a way as to prove the superiority of Catholicism. Each week come one or two new pamphlets, which I must have. I want to get a really complete collection."

"Have you found one on Buddhism?" I inquired. He had not.

"The other reason I go to a Catholic church is that I like the atmosphere in there, that quiet, all those candles and people kneeling at all times absorbed in prayers. There is something in those churches and I like being in them.

"But last week I had a curious experience, really quite curious, I think. I was standing as usual looking at the pamphlet rack when a very old woman came up and thrust one of the pamphlets into my hands. She asked me if I would read it to her as she had left her glasses at home. She then went into the church and knelt in a back pew and I went into the pew with her. She was an old woman, so I couldn't refuse to do as she asked. I read and read for about an hour while the lady made some activity with her beads. I don't believe she heard anything. She was so absorbed in her prayers that she didn't need to listen to my voice. It was nice, it was like going with my mother to a Buddhist temple. In fact, I didn't notice what I was reading myself, in that atmosphere. I have no idea what it was I was reading and though it was rather queer to be going on like that, it really didn't matter at all."

Shimpu's visit to our house on that February day in 1963 was prompted by a discovery he had made the same morning in a Catholic bookstore in Harvard Square.

"*Zen Catholicism!* What do you think of such a practice? And on the back cover, a really fine photograph of a garden. Not a Japanese sort of garden, perhaps, but an elegant garden anyway. A New England Zen garden in a Catholic monastery. There is a photograph of the author, too," and he handed me the book, opened to show the writer, who was described as the Very Reverend Prior of the Benedictine Community on Narragansett Bay and the head of the governing body of the school established by the monastery. He was born in Liverpool in 1907 and became a Benedictine monk in 1930. He spent four years at Oxford and received the S.T.L. degree from the English Dominicans at Blackfriars in 1937. He had traveled and lectured in Canada and the United States. Then there followed an impressive list of the prior's books, as well as articles he had contributed to publications both in the United States and in England.

"What a nice face, a really kind face," I said as I scrutinized the photograph and began to flip through the pages of the book at random. The chapter titles were lively and provocative: "The Importance of Not Being Earnest"; "*Seems,* Madam? Nay, It Is"; "Playing God or Letting God Play?"

"Please do let me borrow it," I said.

"It must be very interesting," said Shimpu. "You can have it for a day or two, as I shall be rather busy."

For two or three days I applied myself to this unusual book and found much that was heartwarming and wise. It was a presentation of Catholicism that was very different from anything I had ever read before, though indeed my knowledge of Catholicism was exceedingly limited. Only one thing bothered and irritated me; the author seemed to feel that Zen could find a place in the Western scheme of things only if it could be subsumed in Catholicism. The dedication of *Zen Catholicism* was "to those who with the insight of the East set in the Great Tradition of the West may even in this painful world be happy." In his conclusion the author wrote: "Whatever be the import of the present widespread interest in Zen, any temptation to Westerners to turn for lasting enlightenment to Japan should be promptly resisted. The evidence points to the discovery of, at best, a mirage."

"Well," I thought, "in a way that is quite true; enlightenment is not a matter of geography, and the Buddha nature is in one's self, whether in England, in the United States, or in Japan." But it did occur to me that Buddhists had been going from one country to another in search of Dharma teachers for two thousand years.

Japanese monks made pilgrimages to China; Korean and Chinese monks went to India. In fact, many perished at sea, in the mountains, and at the hands of brigands while in search of a teacher they hoped would be able to reveal the living meaning of the Buddha's way. The Buddha nature or the Dharma is not the property of any special people or institution; nevertheless, in countries where Buddhism has been practiced for many hundreds of years, sources of inspiration can be found in individuals, or in places like Eihei-ji. These are beacons of encouragement, a necessary source of light strong enough to show up the existence and nature of the eternal Dharma, as well as to stimulate an awareness of the omnipresent shadows of delusion. However, there are many ways in which to become aware of the nature of delusion and self-deception, in which we are all involved. My opportunities while in Japan, as well as with Japanese friends in the United States, to see the Western world through Japanese eyes, both Christian and Buddhist, had been a source of many valuable insights. Now, I wondered, would it also be possible for a Christian monk, a Western roshi or sage, to help one overcome the obstacles to enlightenment and to the realization of one's Buddha nature?

Six years earlier, in 1957, the Cambridge Buddhist Association had been established. A zendo was created in a room of the Italianate house, built in the 1850s, into which we had recently moved. Dr. Shin'ichi Hisamatsu, the first lecturer on Zen Buddhism at the Harvard Divinity School, instructed a small group of us in the practice of zazen. Beginning with some old books from my grandfather's library, as well as a few hundred of my own volumes gathered together during my Harvard years with the help and suggestions of my pupils, a library slowly took shape. The number of people who came to those first zazen sessions was not large; in fact, for a while there were few participants. Lack of a teacher who knew the Western mentality as well as his own religious discipline then seemed to me to be a great handicap. We

Americans are still the spiritual heirs of old Ben Franklin. We are pragmatists, and therefore our first six or seven years of zazen practice almost always involve considerable preoccupation with the questions: Is this really the right practice, the right method for *me*? Isn't the right teacher a sine qua non of practice? I observed that belief in a method or a teacher sometimes became a permanent substitute for actual realization. On the other hand, a restless search for the "best teacher," the "best method," seemed to lead some people only into psychological chaos.

Many Japanese monks and teachers were peregrinating on the east coast of the United States during the late fifties and early sixties. Each had his own way of teaching, his own approach. However, none stayed long enough to establish himself or a rigid method for us, which could have become a crutch on which we might have been unwisely dependent. Japanese monks were, of course, living in California, where they received the financial support of their compatriots' large community, as well as the moral support of their own cultural values. In California the monks were also able to obtain Japanese food. Japanese monks, on the whole, do not care much for American food.

I wondered about the English Catholic monk. Had he made up his mind to finish out his life in the United States in order to teach the values and the discipline of his English Benedictine community? Did he have more rapport with coreligionists of a different nationality than did some Japanese monks? Three or four Japanese teachers living in the United States, I knew, had a wonderful relationship with their Western pupils, by whom they were respected and greatly revered. One roshi in California had worked at all sorts of odd jobs before becoming a full-time teacher. A second teacher would have died of a severe illness in a World War II internment camp had not one of his pupils, a widow, married him, thus effecting his release. He died surrounded by friends and pupils a few months later. However, other roshis were brought to the United States only to find that they could not adapt themselves to the new way of life at all. They refused to study English, to learn anything about America or Americans. Adaptability did not seem to be a matter of age. Some young and middle-aged monks were at least for a time almost neurotically insecure and rigid, while one elderly lay teacher easily settled in with a family in Honolulu and lived happily there for many years, cherished and admired by students of all ages.

"'With regard to Buddhism in Japan,'" read Shimpu from the prior's book, "'in a recent press release from Tokyo, a prominent Buddhist religious leader is quoted as stating: "Unless we adopt the spirit and techniques of Christianity, specifically of the Catholic Church, Japanese Buddhism may soon be a thing of the past. . . . " What this witness has called Christianity's "slow but sure expansion" in Japan has its ironic aspect; it offers little comfort to disaffected Western Christians who might conceivably be seeking to salve their consciences by the cult of Zen on its native soil.'*

"Well," concluded Shimpu, "you have a car; you might drive to see this Zen Catholic monk. You could ask him a lot of questions and tape record his answers for my research."

That was an interesting prospect, to be sure. A number of other points in the book had caught my eye, such as the following: "What is to be done about this ego-awareness, which is a necessity, since without it the individual can achieve little, yet which can torment him almost to the point of wishing for death? The first answer is that nothing can be done about it. If we consciously watch ourselves, strive directly to eliminate egocentric thoughts, the trouble increases, as it would by contemplating one's own unattractiveness in a mirror. The same could be true of a course of asceticism, by which we attempt a violent withdrawal from the objects of craving. Asceticism of itself does not eliminate ego-awareness, rather the reverse. Even prayer and devotion,

*Graham, *Zen Catholicism*, p. 156.

though they can bring us nearer to the root of the matter, have not the power to provide a final solution.

"In a sense there is no final solution. We cannot remove from the human condition what is an integral part of it. But we can, with God's grace (and here, in substance though not in modes of expression, Catholicism and Zen agree), make sense of our self-preoccupation, live with it, and eventually find beatitude through it."*

All this seemed very much in accord with what I had observed in Buddhist monasteries, and particularly with what I had learned about myself from experience in Zen retreats and in Zen meditation.

My opportunity to meet the Zen Catholic Prior came about a year later. God's Motel at Harvard sponsored a series of comparative religion lectures, and an invitation was sent to the Cambridge Buddhist Association.

The first lecture in the series was titled "The Zen Insight and Catholicism." It was to be given by the author of *Zen Catholicism*.

"I'll meet you there," said Shimpu, "and afterwards Dr. Huston Smith, who will certainly be there too, will take you with him to the Motel Master's party. There are always parties in his apartment after lectures. Won't you take a tape recorder? You'll have opportunities to ask some questions."

The small auditorium in God's Motel was crowded the wet February evening that the Zen Catholic Prior was to lecture. The Motel Master introduced the speaker. The prior wore a long black cassock and had a nearly shaven head, all of which gave him a remarkably Buddhist appearance, I thought. In Japan Buddhist monks wear black robes. As Shimpu had foreseen, a party was held after the lecture, and, also as he had foreseen, our mutual friend Huston Smith, professor of philosophy at the Massachusetts Institute of Technology, did take me and kindly

*Graham, *Zen Catholicism*, pp. 68–69.

introduced me to the Zen Catholic priest after the informal discussion period and refreshments were over. I told the priest that I had enjoyed his *Zen Catholicism* and that I would like very much to have an opportunity to ask him some questions about it.

"Well," he said, "I will be here tomorrow. I have been given rooms upstairs, so why don't we have a talk there if you are free and would like to come along sometime in the morning?"

11 SOME QUERIES

*Truly, because of our accepting and rejecting,
we have not the suchness of things.*

                                        Hsinhsinming

W<small>OULD YOU LIKE TO TALK TOGETHER</small> in the auditorium? There are only a few people in there now," the Motel Master inquired of the Zen Catholic monk when I duly arrived for our appointment the following day.

"My room will do nicely," replied the monk. The Motel Master either believed that Catholic monks were terrified of women or that they were great Don Juans. I wore layers of shapeless woollies and my head was wound about in a very long wet scarf, so that I was about as seductive as a soggy teddy bear. It was sleeting heavily outside.

"Well now," began the Prior after we had settled into the bright purple chairs in his comfortable room, about two doors down the corridor from Shimpu's, "you have some questions about *Zen Catholicism?*"

I unwrapped the cold wet scarf from around my head. Suddenly, a moment of near panic! I can't ask him all those questions, I thought. He is a complete stranger and my questions are awfully impertinent. However did I get here? All Shimpu's doing, really, I thought nervously, and the words seemed to stick in hard cold globules under my tongue.

"My host here," began the monk kindly, trying to put me at ease, "tells me that you are a Buddhist. Surely you were something before you became a Buddhist."

"I was a skeptic, I guess," I replied lamely.

"Were you christened that way . . . ?"

"Oh, I wasn't ever christened. But I have taken part in a Tokudo ceremony in which water is sprinkled on one's head— didn't the custom originate in India?—and which attaches my karma to Buddhism and to a Buddhist teacher. A Zen teacher, actually."

"In this initiation did you make any promises? Surely Zennists don't accept any creeds."

"One goes to the Buddhas and Patriarchs 'for refuge.' Then one promises to try to follow the Precepts—which actually brings me to one of the questions I had in mind to ask." Courage and warmth seemed to be returning simultaneously. "In *Zen Catholicism* you wrote that people who practice Zen 'have a tendency to sit lightly to ethical obligations and even seek to rationalize this irresponsibility by an appeal to an implied philosophy of Buddhism.' Do you really think Christians are more ethical? Do all of the Catholics you know keep the Ten Commandments better than your Zen friends keep to their *Kai*, their Precepts?"

"Well now," he said laughing, "maybe you are the one to give me an answer to that question. Offhand I don't remember any mention of Precepts in the books of Dr. Daisetz Suzuki, or of some of the Western writers whom one reads on Zen. Of course I know that the Buddhism of the Theravadin has Precepts to be followed. Dr. Suzuki and Mr. Watts, who write so much about Zen, tell us about nondualism, pure experience, satori, enlightenment. . . ."

I had to admit that Dr. Suzuki did not go into the ethical aspect of Zen and that even the Zen scholar R. H. Blyth, who had lived in Zen temples, did not include any discussion of Precepts or Precept-taking ceremonies in those of his books that I had read.

"Were the kamikaze pilots Buddhists, do you think?" inquired the Prior. Later I learned that his mother had been killed by a German bomb during World War II.

"The only ex-kamikaze pilot I have met," I said, "became interested in Zen after the war was over. He participated in a Precept-taking ceremony, then he decided to renounce drinking and all forms of violence, even fishing and hunting. It is impossible to be a Buddhist and take any life for sport or for amusement."

"Did he regret that he had not died, a hero, in combat?"

"He said that you cannot fight a war and think; thinking and fighting are incompatible. Had the war lasted one more day, he told me, his turn to end his life in a plane would have come and he wouldn't be alive now to practice Zen. When the war ended he began to do a lot of thinking. Too much, in fact, and he became an alcoholic. Zen meditation cured him of alcoholism, and he doesn't want to kill anyone or anything now."

"That's very nice, and very much in the spirit of the Buddha," said the Prior.

"The title of one of your chapters in *Zen Catholicism* interested me," I said. "It is 'With Firmness in the Right.' Of course there are commandments and precepts, and probably most people do their best to follow them according to their own lights. But life is complicated and really knowing right and wrong is enormously difficult, perhaps impossible in the long run. At least that is how it seems to me."

"It is also difficult for Christians," he said.

"In *Zen Catholicism* you invite Zennists, whether Oriental or Occidental, to give their account of the content of the word 'ought' . . ."

"Yes, perhaps you would like to tell me something about that. Do some Zennists follow the Noble Eightfold Path? Possibly that is their 'ought'?"

"Our 'ought' is enlightened understanding of the Precepts; this actually involves their interpretation. Do you think any precept or commandment can be applied to a specific situation without any interpretation whatsoever?" The Prior agreed that no commandment or precept could be put into actual practice without some degree of interpretation.

"One tries to live in the light of the Holy Spirit, to act as far as possible without egotism," he said. Then he inquired if Zen spontaneity didn't tend to lead to egotism. I admitted that a lot of very tiresome behavior was probably justified in the name of Zen spontaneity, but that Buddhists who practiced zazen tried to live in accord with their Buddha nature.

"There are even special koans which deal with the Precepts and teach one to interpret them *mushin,* that is, egolessly."

The Prior then told me that he would be leaving the United States to return to England in a year or two and that he hoped to return to his country by way of Asia. He said he wished to see something of the Buddhist tradition and to meet some Buddhist personalities. My heart sank at that proposal. I had read too many accounts written by Christian clergymen who, after benefiting from Buddhist hospitality, had returned to their own countries, only to write smug and patronizing books or articles about the superiority of Christianity, seen with their own eyes, in "heathen" lands.

"It is hard to see Buddhism in Japan," I said, "except for a few temples which specialize in making money off tourists. Many of the best roshis, old teachers, speak no English. Buddhist temples are very cold and damp, and there are no beds or chairs. You would be terribly uncomfortable, I think."

The Prior smiled. "It sounds as though you're trying to discourage me!"

"Well, yes, I suppose I am. In fact, I hope you will decide to visit some Christian countries on your way home. It is really impossible to understand someone else's religion by reading about it and by just looking in from the outside. Besides, it is part of Christian doctrine that other religions are inadequate and inferior. So why do Christians bother about other religions at all?" Water was beginning to seep through my boots and my feet were becoming icy cold.

"I think Christians have a great deal to learn from the Zen intuition; there is much I would like to learn," he said patiently.

"But you would see everything through Christian eyes, and it just wouldn't be any use," I protested. I could feel my face becoming rather warm, and I added hastily, "I am sorry, I really didn't mean to say exactly that—" He smiled warmly. "I am glad you said it, and I am interested in everything you have to tell me." Curiously, I was sure this was not just politeness, that he really was interested. He was an attentive listener. Time had slid by very fast, and suddenly he looked at his watch, remarking that his train left in about an hour. He would have to pack.

"But one thing I would like to ask first," he said. "What do you consider the heart of Zen? Are there just a few lines you can quote that really seem to you to be at the heart of the matter?"

"Well—Zen is Buddhism and Buddhism is so many things. They are all necessary and all hang together—but the four vows of the Bodhisattva are absolutely indispensable to the spirit of Zen." I then repeated for him the four-line vow:

"Sentient beings are countless, vow to enlighten them.

"Suffering is endless, vow to relieve it.

"The Dharma is infinite, vow to practice it.

"The way of the Buddha goes on forever, vow to follow it."

"And that is Zen, is it? Well, this has been a very interesting talk. However, possibly you have some other questions in mind. I am sorry that I have no time to go into them today."

"Maybe I could write them to you in a letter?" I queried.

"I have no time for correspondence," the Prior said firmly. "However, if you will come to the priory some afternoon, we can have tea together. I will be pleased to talk with you again."

As I left, I gave him an envelope containing some of the literature of the Cambridge Buddhist Association. It seemed an importunate gesture, but I thought it might open up further avenues of thought and conversation. At least I hoped it might, despite a few passing reflections on the rather unfruitful nature of my early encounters with Christianity.

I remembered rather uneasily the conventional Christianity that many traditional Bostonians embrace. Episcopalianism is one of the most fashionable Boston religious institutions. "That is a good church to join if you want to adopt good-caliber children," someone once told us, rather conjuring up visions of foundlings housed in expensive Skinner boxes labeled Grade A, Grade B, and so forth. "You can always drop the church membership after the adoptions have become final." Some of my relatives were Episcopalians. They were careful to baptize their children with the local spring water (possibly it had powers to hold the local gremlins and evil spirits in abeyance), and they forgathered whenever practicable in family pews furbished with highly polished nameplates. Japanese people attend the temple where the family *ihai*, or death plaques, are kept. My Boston relatives sit in pews with little polished bronze plaques bearing the names of their ancestors. Ancestor worship seems to be at the heart of the religion of all conventional people, whatever their creed or ethnic status.

Once a rather churchy cousin visited us and, on seeing a photograph album on the table, asked to be shown our pictures. I turned the pages, happy with an opportunity to share my color photos of good friends and nostalgic scenery in Japan.

"Oh I'm not interested in all of *that*," exclaimed the churchy person. "I only want to see pictures of brother's children! Find those for me, please."

"These wonderful Christians, they love mankind and humanity. They will support endless good works in the name of their religion, but they are only really interested in their own friends and kinfolk," I said to Jack. "That's what bibliolatry, all those begats and begats, does for them!"

"Well," said Jack, "one should really feel sorry for people who must spend so much of their lives closed in their Sunday boxes and subjected to endless harangues, to begats and begats, in order to reassure themselves that they are indeed the 'chosen ones' on the threshold of a promised land. In Austria people get up and walk out during the sermon if it is too long or if they don't like it. They can return after the talk is over, in time for communion."

༄

Only one member of my family was a Roman Catholic, a distant cousin who was a convert. He lived in England. Once while Jack and I were in London, my father-in-law hired a great old-fashioned ark of a prewar car and we set out on an expedition through the countryside to the county of Gloucestershire. We had decided to visit this Catholic cousin of my maternal grandmother, who lived in Chipping Campden in an Elizabethan house around which he had created a world-famous garden. (This unique garden is described in a beautifully illustrated book by Peter Coats, *Great Gardens of the Western World*.) My cousin's address had been given to me by one of my aunts just before we left the States. "Do go to see Laurie," she urged, "even though he may not know who you are. A bomb landed too close to him while he was an air-raid warden, and he has forgotten so many things and probably even many of us." One matter he

SOME QUERIES   161

was said to have forgotten was his youthful conversion to Roman Catholicism, and the Sunday Masses in the small chapel adjoining his house had had to be discontinued because neither priest nor friends were able to awaken in him any memory of his spiritual home.

At Hidcote Manor, in the quiet Cotswold hills, we were met at the door by a rather surly manservant. Upon being told that I was a relative he vanished, then returned accompanied by a nursing sister, a pink-cheeked countrywoman. She ushered us into a room with an enormous fireplace.

The master of the house was recovering from shingles, and therefore only I was invited to visit with him in his upstairs apartment. My husband and in-laws were provided tea and the companionship of the sister before the comfortable hearth downstairs.

My elderly cousin, Lawrence Johnstone, received me in a large room filled with heavy Queen Anne furniture. Seven very small dachshunds rushed to greet me with surprising friendliness. Cousin Laurie had the classic profile of my mother's family. In spite of his indisposition, he was carefully dressed in well-cut tweeds. He was obviously delighted to meet me: "You must be Julie's daughter," he said. This would have made me my own mother. I tried to explain, but time had more or less stopped for him a generation earlier. This experience of a shift in time gears was neither unpleasant nor uncomfortable. The old gentleman's presence wove an atmosphere of warmth and serenity around the large solid furnishings and the many old books in these bachelor quarters. Tea and hot biscuits were brought by the valet. An invisible sun lit the quiet room, and the cold, wet day seemed in retreat far beyond the heavy polished woodwork. The old gentleman described his journeys into Himalayan mountain forests and some of the botanical discoveries he had made there. As he described these quests and the infinite variety of extraordinary flora and fauna he had observed, it became evident that his search for beauty went far beyond a preoccupation with phenomena and scenery.

Finally he said, "Come, I must show you around. You have come so far, and we may not have an opportunity to meet again. This place is no longer mine. I have given it over to the National Trust and they allow me to live in a few of the rooms for five months each year." He led me through large empty rooms, where all was covered with sheets and tarpaulins, then through a bathroom with the Battle of Waterloo depicted on the ceramic tiles. At last we went downstairs, where I introduced him to my in-laws, and together we walked out into the garden. The afternoon was cold and sunless. Though the giant box and grass were green, there were no flowers, and many of the bushes were still brown and bare. The walk led us through the box-lined outdoor "rooms," down one of the long grass avenues that fanned out in a star shape from the central enclosure. At the end of the long grass stretch was an Orientally inspired pavilion. A tall wrought-iron gate opened out, so it appeared, into the heavens. Beyond the gate nothing could be seen but pale clouds in the leaden sky.

Cousin Laurie bent over and gently stroked the bare limb of a small bush as though it were a favorite cat or dog. "A garden is a metaphysical creation," he reflected thoughtfully. "But is it the metaphysic which creates the garden, or the garden the metaphysic?"

As he accompanied us through the courtyard to bid us goodbye, we passed the chapel, which stood at right angles to the house.

"Is it used now?" I asked, indicating the chapel.

"Probably something was done in it once a very long time ago," he remarked absently. "Look, look how small it is; they use it for a toolshed now," and he opened the door to show us. A white pigeon flew up onto a beam above our heads. We stood looking up at that white bird for a few very quiet minutes. Then cousin Laurie said, "Birds like it in here; it is full of nests and eggs hidden round about. My gardeners would like to clean them all out, but they'll never do that while I am here. People, birds, and gardens all need each other! If only a way could be found to make more people realize this."

It has always seemed to me that though this charming and courtly old man had forgotten so much, possibly he had remembered something of ultimate importance. Names, times, dates, places, we are constantly forgetting them and in the end we forget them all. For those in search of the ultimate, at least a temporary forgetting precedes the deepest insights into the nature of things. If cousin Laurie forgot his Catholicism, possibly this was because the version of that religion which he had embraced in his youth involved a suffocating preoccupation with too many shallow and rigid rules and formulae. On the other hand, his long endeavors to coax life and beauty from what had once been windswept Cotswold fields, his mountain pilgrimages, and finally, the bomb that nearly took his life possibly had brought him closer to the heart of the matter, perhaps even to a glimpse of the great Void. According to a Buddhist tradition, a Moon-faced Buddha's awakening is of one day's and one night's duration. A long life and a deep awakening are the fruits of good karma; but so too is a short life blessed by even a few moments of illumination.

Sometimes I wondered about my elderly cousin and about his forgotten creed. Certainly the faith of my former pupil, the old Russian colonel, had impressed me deeply. I often thought of him sitting under his icon with his little paintbrushes and flowers, and decided that possibly there was something to be learned about Christianity from the Benedictine monk and from his *Zen Catholicism,* should an opportunity arise.

12 LEX ORANDI, LEX CREDENDI

The believing mind is the Buddha nature.
Nirvana Sutra

A WEEK OR SO AFTER our meeting at Harvard, I received a kind letter from the Prior, in which he thanked me for the gift of reading material that I had given him as we parted. He wrote that he particularly appreciated a small pamphlet on the Zen practice of meditation for beginners written by my Buddhist teacher, Rindo Fujimoto Roshi. The Prior concluded by saying that our talk had been the occasion of new insights and he would be happy to see me again should I ever find myself in the vicinity of his priory. Thus, despite his protestation of lack of time for correspondence, a correspondence did indeed develop. I sent him one or two reviews of his *Zen Catholicism* that I had found in Japanese publications. I also tried to explain why I felt that Christian monks were somewhat less than welcome in Japan. I found a few books on Buddhism by Christian scholars in the library of the Cambridge Buddhist Association and copied some excerpts, such as the following by a famous French scholar: Buddhism "is not only to be set aside as less beautiful or less efficient . . . it is to be rejected as an abomination,"* wrote this clerical gentleman in his *La Rencontre du Bouddhisme et de l'Occident.* I added that the book was in many Buddhist libraries, so I was grateful that comparatively few Japanese scholars were fluent enough in French to read it.

The Prior replied: "I quite understand and fully sympathize with the attitude of representative Buddhists to receiving Christian ministers. Though oddly enough, for some reason or other, I have never conceived of myself as falling within that category! Despite your charming attempts to warn me off, I still hope to see something of Buddhism in its own setting before I die."

In the early part of May, about three months after our first meeting, I decided to pay a visit to an aunt who lived not very far from the monastery of the Zen Catholic Prior. The Prior invited me to hear a Mass sung in the priory church and to have tea in the rooms of one of the monks, the monk who had designed the unique New England Zen garden that was on the dust jacket of *Zen Catholicism.*

Just before my departure for the visit, it occurred to me that perhaps I might present the Zen Catholic Prior with one of the scrolls that my husband and I had acquired in Japan some years earlier. His mind seemed quite set on that visit to Japanese Buddhist temples. If he couldn't be dissuaded from the project, perhaps he could be coaxed into seeing Buddhism through Buddhist eyes, if only a little. The Mahayana scriptures maintained that all men have the Buddha nature; the problem is how to awaken it. Zen masters believe that one way is the contemplation of calligraphy. I decided to give the Prior an eighteenth-century Chinese calligraphy scroll. The vigorous characters were alive

*Henri de Lubac, *La Rencontre du Bouddhisme et de l'Occident* (Paris, Aubier, 1952), p. 279.

and the work of a strong, sure hand. The characters read: "Walking along Lake Dotei, hearing the sound of the soundless iron flute." I tucked the fragile wooden box with its rolled-up scroll under my arm and set out for the Buddhist-Catholic encounter.

This Prior obviously was a very special person. He appeared to me to possess a high degree of enlightenment, of a Christian nature. I felt that he was one who had made the long painful journey into the dragon's cave, down to the bottom of the mind, in his own Christian way. There was, in his manner, the warmth, light, and quiet assurance I had found to be characteristic of the best Japanese roshis I had met. There was also the quiet simplicity, the gentle, playful humor. Well, we would see how things developed.

The priory was located on the top of a hill overlooking a large bay. The approach led through a country lane on either side of which cows were grazing in the fields. It was a bright spring day. A sharp salt wind blew through the small pine and cryptomeria trees surrounding the monastery and school buildings. The church, very large for a school chapel, I thought, was Byzantine in shape, but the proportions and use of dark stained wood in combination with New England fieldstone conveyed a very Japanese feeling. I parked the car and sat watching a black-robed figure oversee the planting of a large Japanese pine. The root ball had to be set in an enormous hole at just the correct angle to show off the interesting shapes of the green-needled branches to advantage.

I had arrived nearly half an hour early for my rendezvous, not wishing to lose my way and thereby arrive late. I decided to look inside the church on my way to the monastery. Monastery and church were joined by a long cloister. Just in front of the monastery, beneath the church, was the Zen garden with New England stones carefully set in raked sand. A flowering azalea and a cedar tree drew the eye into the heart of the garden. The church stood on a high stone foundation and was entered through heavy bronze-plated oak doors that were difficult to open against the sea wind. Inside, a subdued blue and gold light streamed through the windows onto the stone floor and the austere altar, surmounted by a modern abstract image of the Christian Messiah suspended from shimmering golden streamers. The church was empty, so by a small side altar where there were no seats I decided to sit for a little time in the style in which one sits in Japanese temples, that is, on my heels. I remained there for about twenty minutes. The church was new and full of hope. The soft weathered stones, homilies of porous strength, attested to a tradition both open and secure. Before leaving, I lit a candle and dedicated a Buddhist dharani to—I was not sure What or Whom. It was an aspiration, a hope of communion.

The Prior came to greet me in the visitors' room outside his office. "Women," he said cheerfully, "cannot go inside the monastery, except for the wife of the governor or of the president of the United States." I couldn't decide just what this said for the wives of officials, or the monks' views thereof. Rather hesitantly, I presented my offering, which, I was delighted to find, was very acceptable to the reverend gentleman. In fact the scroll, now framed, hangs in his room at Ampleforth Abbey in England, where presently he lives in retirement. His most recent book includes a photograph on the dust jacket of the author seated in front of the vigorously painted Chinese characters.

"I have decided to try to learn something about your religion, Catholicism," I told him and added that also I wished to find out more about how Buddhist and Zen intuitions might be developed within the Western tradition. I said that I had bought the paperback edition of one of his earlier books, *The Love of God*, and that though it was very interesting, I had no doctrinal background whereby really to benefit from the book.

After about half an hour of conversation, the Prior guided me to one of the school dormitories, where the creator of the Zen garden, a housemaster, resided. As I was ushered into this personage's apartment, which adjoined the dormitory, a tall black-robed figure appeared carrying an enormous tray of tea things.

"So this is the Zen lady," he said, peering down over the tea tray. "You don't look like one. . . . Aren't Zen people supposed to be hairless?" His dog, a Scottish border collie, sidled up wagging his tail in a most amiable way.

"He is a Presbyterian," said the robed figure, putting down the tray, on which were all sorts of delicacies. The Prior informed me that these were all concocted in the reverend father's bathroom, in his shower.

"Father is an artist: churches, gardens, cooking! All of the trees and plants so beautifully set out around our new church and monastery, all of them are the fruits of his labors and of his talents." The venerable gentleman was warmly hospitable; his kindness had a Buddhist simplicity that I found very appealing. Some time later the Prior told me: "Father has many visitors because though he is one of the busiest monks in our community, he always has time for people's troubles, all kinds of difficulties, students' problems, married people's troubles, all sorts of family fusses. Anything that a person considers a problem, he, or she, for that matter, comes along and talks about it, and father always listens. Then he provides tea, or if time permits, a beautiful meal. His friends leave feeling stronger and happier, knowing that someone understood their feelings and cared."

The Presbyterian licked my hand and turned his worshipful gaze in the direction of his owner. He obviously approved of the approval of his lord and master.

"You are a Bostonian," said the reverend artist, handing me an enormous teacup full of strong tea. "I have known some Bostonians, and there is really no one like them. Years ago, I knew an elderly Boston woman who joined some kind of Indian religion. She was interested in me because I was the only Catholic priest she had ever met. We got on very well, and, in fact, a relative of hers who didn't have much use for Indian religion once asked me to have a talk with her—I couldn't imagine why. 'You really must speak to so-and-so,' said the relative. 'She is getting *so* eccentric and her income just isn't up to it!' "

The Presbyterian sat looking out the screen door at a large seagull who was drinking water from a metal dogdish, his dish, while three or four other gulls squatted on the grass close by.

Before my departure from the priory, I returned to the church for the midday Mass. I had always loved Gregorian chant and plainsong, and this was the first time I had ever been present while they were being sung. I could not help thinking that if Christians were to base their claims to truth on the numinous quality, the sacred "Emptiness," evoked by their contemplatively sung chant or by a contemplative Latin Mass, I might have been persuaded that, on the whole, Catholicism was indeed the best way for most Westerners to seek the truth. However, a church stripped to its preoccupation with uniqueness, with history, to proclamations and programs for righteousness, no matter how necessary or commendable these may be, is neither suasive nor appealing. The path to truth and enlightenment is difficult, discouraging, and full of pitfalls. Without meditation or a truly contemplative liturgy to clear the mind and evoke the timeless, the numinous, it seems to me that institutional religion is far more a deterrent than an assistance to the life of the spirit.

During the communion of the Mass in the Zen Catholic monastery, I made the unexpected discovery that the "Emptiness" of the zazen mental discipline, which the atmosphere of this church quickly induced, rendered the Christian mystery wholly present and infinitely desirable. "Like swimming in the heart of the sun," as Thomas Merton has so beautifully expressed it. It was as strange as it was unexpected, this experience, and in retrospect I was uncomfortable about it, nor was I sure how to deal with it.

Some years later, I discovered that my experience was not unique. In reading through the transcript of a conversation that the Prior had had with a German Jesuit, a longtime resident in Japan who had had much experience in zazen, I learned that the German priest was not unfamiliar with the phenomenon. This priest told the Prior that a year earlier his church had been visited by an old lady who had been practicing zazen for many years. She told the German that zazen was very good and important but that she greatly missed the presence of ceremonies, of ritual, in celebration of the divine. Ironically, some recently organized or even Western-influenced zazen groups are run on the principle that ritual and chanting are unmodern and unintellectual, and that a practice of zazen-only is a really pure, updated Zen. Zen as practiced in traditional temples is always accompanied by chanting and traditional Buddhist ceremony. The German priest's elderly visitor inquired if she might attend the Mass held every morning after the zazen practice in the priest's church. He replied that she was always welcome at Mass. Three months later the old lady asked to join the Catholic church. As the priest remarked to the Prior, she had found her own way into the church without any indoctrination efforts or arguments. Wasn't this "not playing God, but letting God play"?

A day or so after my visit to the Zen Catholic Prior in his monastery, while I was immersed in the intricacies of his very orthodox first book, *The Love of God,* I received the following letter:

13 May 1964

Dear Elsie,

I have to be away from here for three or four days next week, so I thought I would drop you a little line (a) to thank you for coming to visit and also (b) to say how deeply appreciative I am for that beautiful Chinese scroll. It is now hanging in my study—a joy to the eye and (thanks to your explanatory material now posted on the card and hidden behind the scroll) meaningful indeed. I am being repeatedly visited by Christian monks anxious to see it!

A nice young Japanese Jesuit has been here twice to talk with me. He is entranced with the scroll and says that, being an original, it is most precious! He is also fascinated by the actual koan. I said that I expected him to unfold it to me. At which he laughed. He is quiet and composed, full of humor and generally good to be with. Yesterday he talked to me about the koan in a way that conveyed a real intuition to me. His Catholic theological interests are much the same as my own, and I think he has reached to the heart of the spiritual life. He deplores that Japanese Catholicism is so "Western" and regards it as his main problem: how to express Catholic philosophy in the Japanese idiom.

To add a few words to our discussion about *Zen Catholicism*. I did not expect that the book would attract much attention among Buddhists and (after having seen at least one Buddhist review) I am rather sorry that it has, as I do not feel qualified to address them. No, my book was written chiefly for Catholics or Christians in general, or Western "neutrals," to bring them something of what I understand to be the basic "insight" of the East, which Westerners need, just as Easterners need perhaps something from the West.

I would not advise you to struggle very hard with my *The Love of God*. It was written more than 25 years ago and accentuates a frame of thought considerably different from what now occupies my mind.

Maybe we will have another opportunity to talk about this and related matters before too long. Come again some time that is convenient for you.

With every best wish,

Gratefully yours,
The Zen Catholic Prior

Our third meeting took place in Cambridge toward the end of May. I met the Prior at the train in Boston, then drove him to Cambridge, where he had tea with me and my husband. Jack was just home from the hospital, recuperating from mononucleosis. The Prior was much interested in Zen meditation, about which we had already had some discussion. I told him that it was a source of disappointment and frustration to me that I was unable to return to Japan for further meditation instruction and for retreats with my Japanese Buddhist teacher, Rindo Fujimoto Roshi. I told the Prior that I was in fairly regular communication with the old Japanese teacher and that he always offered encouragement, that he wrote urging me to be patient and to continue the practice of zazen by myself, as well as in the sessions of the Cambridge Buddhist Association.

The Prior found the zazen, which I described to him, rather austere. He said he practiced a sort of yoga meditation himself each day, but sitting for three-quarters of an hour daily, not to mention eight hours during retreat, seemed long to him. He felt that fifteen or twenty minutes each session was probably enough for most people.

After his visit to us in Cambridge, the Prior wrote:

22 May 1964

Dear Elsie,

Thank you for your very kind letter which came this morning. One of life's little puzzles to me is that so many good humans living in "the world" seem to want to become more and more monastic whereas I, a happy monk, want to become more fully human. But perhaps it's not so strange after all.

I did enjoy my visit with you and your husband. All the sentient beings in your home pleased me: the humans, the dogs, the cat, and the large luxurious plant. I was most grateful for the visit and your kind hospitality.

Perhaps you will tell your English friend, the one whose

letter you showed me, that I think there is no danger of the Catholic church making any "take over bid" towards Zen. In which connection I share Baron Von Hügel's view, that if I could make a convert by getting up and walking across the room, I would not do so. Conversions, where they are genuine, are entirely an affair of the Holy Spirit.

The other day I was visited by a Mr. Holmes Hinkley Welch, a Harvard "Associate in Research, Chinese Buddhism." He lives in Concord, Massachusetts, and describes himself as "cold roast Boston." The point of his visit here was to leave me a very interesting manuscript of a book he is writing on Chinese Buddhist monasteries, not that I could contribute any scholarship, but to save him from any "howlers" from the Western point of view. His book is quite fascinating and we spent two hours going over it, very profitable for me. Meeting Mr. Welch as well as you and your husband makes me want to meet more Buddhists, conscious or unconscious, professed or unprofessed. It even makes me wonder whether a "Zen Catholic" such as I (presumably, or at least arguably) am could be eligible as a sort of honorary member of your Buddhist Association? But most probably, from your point of view, which is the decisive one in this case, it does not make any sense at all.

Mr. Welch's book, which describes at length what goes on in a Buddhist meditation hall, seemed to throw a lot of light on a number of points we touched lightly on in our last conversation. Is the pressure too high? Shouldn't one take a slowly worked out lifetime to reach what I take to be the calmness of Enlightenment, and not force the pace? But I do not profess to know. I must show you a little book on "solitude" which Thomas Merton has just sent to me.

Say a little (Buddhist?) prayer for me sometimes.

Very sincerely,
The Zen Catholic Prior

Thanks to the Prior's kindness, Holmes Welch and I were introduced. Mr. Welch, the author of a wise and whimsical little book on Taoism and, later, three learned volumes on Chinese Buddhism,* was indeed to become a good friend, as well as the vice-president of the Cambridge Buddhist Association.

To the Prior's inquiry about the possibility of his joining the Buddhist Association, I wrote him that already there were a number of non-Buddhist members who joined simply because they liked our way of meditation or because they wanted to use the library, which had been developed into quite a good collection over a period of eight years.

However, I inquired rashly, wouldn't the Prior be ex-communicated should he participate in Buddhist meditation or the chanting of Buddhist sutras that takes place before and after meditation sessions?

In order to learn more about Catholicism I decided to sub-scribe to a Catholic magazine. The articles were varied, and the perspective was not too rigidly dogmatic. With the subscription, I received gratis from the publishers a small black book, *The Divine Office*. I wrote to the Prior: "I have just started to read *The Divine Office*, a book sent to me by the Catholic magazine, *Jubilee*, to which I told you I have taken out a subscription. The little book has a beautiful dust cover, a photograph of Notre Dame à Strasbourg." I opened the book at random and read the following:

Christ's Victory
I ground them fine as the dust before the wind
like the mud in the streets I trampled them down.

This remarkable psalm continues:

The Practice of Chinese Buddhism: 1900–1950 (Cambridge, Massachusetts, Harvard University Press, 1967), *The Buddhist Revival in China* (Harvard University Press, 1968), and *Buddhism Under Mao* (Harvard University Press, 1972).

The Head of Pagan Nations
A people I had not known became my slaves;
As soon as they heard me they obeyed.
The foreigners fawned and cringed
before me; they staggered forth from their fortresses.

To the Prior I quoted these verses and added that to this pagan mind it occurred that the foregoing lines would sound somewhat better in Latin. And if non-Christians were to come "staggering forth from their fortresses," I hoped it would not be to embrace such ferocious sentiments as these! "Don't you think," I wrote, "that *Jubilee* might turn up a less formidable introduction to circulate among the heathens? Why don't they just send around the nice picture on the dust jackets and keep the little black books for their own private inspiration? I hope you are not offended, I am sure the editors of *Jubilee* had the most charitable of intentions and their book has a very elegant binding. . . ."
The Prior replied:

6 June 1964

Dear Elsie,
If I were to practice zazen with your group I should not be in the least danger of "excommunication" because I should, or could, only do so according to the principles of my *Zen Catholicism,* which is a thoroughly orthodox Catholic book. Which leads me to say that I don't feel it would be a success if I joined the Buddhists in their ritual, other than by sitting and being absolutely quiet. That is how I practice zazen meditation twice a day here at the monastery, quietly, alone, and as a conclusion to a little series of yoga exercises which raise the level of consciousness quite remarkably. And my "Dharanis", when I use any, are "Jesus", or "God be praised", or "Lord have mercy on me a sinner", or something equally Christian, according to the principle:

lex orandi, lex credendi, the way of believing is the way of praying. All of which, according to my understanding, is perfectly compatible with the acceptance of the Buddha's Holy Truths. So maybe I misled you by my inquiry about joining your association. Were the opportunity to arise, I should like to be with (i.e. "associate with") Buddhists for a time: but rather informally than formally, exchanging thoughts maybe a little, but preferably not in high powered academic discussions, for which I do not have much capacity or taste.

Do I convey to you the impression of being frenetically interested in Old Testament pronouncements which, I cordially agree, often seem dramatically noisy? I suggest that you write to *Jubilee*. They would be glad to publish your letter. Explain that you have aired this particular grievance to a Catholic priest friend and that he has grown weary of pointing out that lots of the Old Testament is junk, that it represents Bronze Age religion, that the brightest of the church fathers did not take much of it seriously, turning it into mere allegory (so Origen, Ambrose, Augustine), and that the aforesaid priest friend no longer takes these complaints seriously but regards them as little ploys by a female gadfly!

I have no time for more.

God bless you.

Very sincerely,
Your Zen Catholic Prior

My correspondence with the Prior became quite regular, and we exchanged letters about once a week. I sent him new books on Buddhism; he lent me books on various aspects of Catholicism, including a number by the late Thomas Merton, a friend of his, and also by another English Benedictine writer, Dom Bede Griffiths. Father Griffiths wrote a sort of autobiography on how he became a Catholic through an interest in Hinduism, which seemed to evolve into questions about history and, as I wrote to the Prior, considerable preoccupation with who has the right answer to it all, that is, who is sitting in the right pew.

The Prior and I had had several discussions on the Christian philosophy of history and on eschatology. Eschatology, the Prior told me, is a theory of the last things, when history draws to a conclusion and all has been perfected by a God of wisdom and love. "Some theologians," said the Prior, "believe that the great contribution the West could make to the East is the doctrine of eschatology. In Tennyson's words: 'one far-off divine event, to which the whole creation moves'!"

An interesting theory, I reflected. However, this would be a dubious contribution, to judge from past Western efforts, both religious and secular, to hustle along the coming of the big event, to hustle creation into utopias and gardens of Eden. Wasn't it just this obsession with manipulating creation that had brought about such horrendous eruptions of intolerance and bloodshed throughout Western history? This deity of Christian history seemed to me a *deus ex machina*. Furthermore, I was not persuaded that Christians cultivated a historical point of view at all. When and where was it possible to draw a definite line between myth and history? However, it seemed unlikely that history would become, in Paul Tillich's phrase, a "broken myth" for a people preoccupied with being the "chosen" of God.

Among Buddhists, becoming unduly engrossed in perfectibility and future events is considered a delusion. It is also thought to be a harmful distraction from tasks at hand. At worst, it is a hindrance to enlightenment. The Bodhisattva Maitreya, who will be the Buddha of a future era of peace and blessedness, receives little attention from present-day Buddhists. Contemplation of future states of bliss could be a great consolation in times of stress and misfortune. However, would such contemplation lead to a wider realization of the Buddha nature?

13 SEPARATE VESSELS

Seeking the mind with the mind—
is not this the greatest of all mistakes?
                                    Hsinhsinming

IN JULY OF 1964, Jack and I invited the Prior to visit us for a few days in our house on Cape Cod. One night was to be spent in my parents' house in Milton, a suburb of Boston, and then we were to proceed to the Cape the following morning. We planned to meet at the priory, in front of the church. While I was awaiting the Prior there, I noticed the monk who had created the Zen garden at work weeding the heather that grew on the slope in front of the church. It was a very hot day; the monk wore Bermuda shorts and was shirtless. I approached and greeted him. He said a few words and quickly returned to his weeding.

"Do you approve of having your prior spend a few days with heathens?" I inquired.

"Oh," he replied, "I think it's a splendid idea—" However, I didn't think he sounded exactly convinced. Well, I thought to myself, a good many strange things have been written in newspapers and journals in the wake of those self-incinerations by Buddhist monks in Vietnam. He probably thinks that even American Buddhists are rather odd and lead a decidedly singular sort of existence.

After the Prior had attended to some appointments in Boston, I drove him to my family's house in Milton. We arrived shortly after supper. My mother was in Maine, and my father had gone to spend a few hours with one of his sisters, who lived a few miles away. The Prior retired to bed with a book on Buddhism, and I took our two dogs for a short walk in the woods behind the house. The following morning I awoke early and found the Prior already in the dining room waiting for the housekeeper to bring his breakfast. We had hardly said good morning when my father strode briskly into the room. My father, at sixty-nine, was exceedingly vigorous and active, both mentally and physically. He is forthright and always says exactly what is on his mind. The Prior rose and introduced himself amiably. Father shook hands. He sat down, studied his cereal thoughtfully for a minute or so. Then he turned to the Prior, who was just reaching for his freshly poured coffee, and inquired: "Well now, does one address you as reverend, as sir, or as padre? What is expected?" The Prior replied that he would answer (and had answered) to quite a number of labels but that he thought padre was rather nice.

"All right, padre," said father, "now that we have this settled, I have an important question to put to you, a matter which has puzzled me for quite a number of years!"

"Yes," said the Prior.

"Will you," said father, "will you please be good enough to tell me why, why ever in the world, my daughter should find it necessary to be a vegetarian?" The Prior's coffee was cold before the explanation was finished. It was a very good explanation involving the Buddhist sentiment that one should strive to limit the amount of suffering and death that existence itself inevitably entails, a sort of existential noblesse oblige. I could not have given such a good explication had the question been put to me, which it had not. At least not by my father. I learned later that the Prior was not at all fond of vegetables except for peas and cauliflower; he far preferred to eat meat. Animals are "raised up" by human consumption, according to orthodox Catholic doctrine.

The Prior loved the Cape, and our quiet life there, without cocktail parties or other social activities, seemed to please him. He rose very early each morning to say his office and rosary. Followed by one of our two large dogs, he would quietly leave the house (in all kinds of weather except a downpour) and walk slowly around the terrace overlooking the ocean. At first our dog Olaf was puzzled by the walk. It had no destination. He watched the procedure attentively. Olaf is an unusual dog, who on the whole prefers watching things to smelling them. He watches boats, birds, and insects, sometimes for hours at a time. But above all, Olaf is an enthusiastic people-watcher. After surveying the Prior's early-morning ritual, he finally decided that those walks, though they had no visible destination, were the source of an attractive aura of peace and good will. So while the office was being read and the rosary repeated, he walked quietly behind. Round and round and round.

The second day of his first Cape visit with us the Prior told me that he would like to practice Zen meditation with me. At that time, I sat cross-legged on the floor for about forty minutes each day. So we sat together and I was aware of the quietness, of what he called the True Self. It filled the small room where we sat together in our respective forms of meditation. At the conclusion of the meditation, I silently said a short dharani. I think he too said a prayer silently. Though our prayers were different, we always felt a sense of communion after these short sessions. I was grateful for this compassionate and wordless encouragement, especially as my health was deteriorating again. Fevers and pains were a frequent source of frustration and annoyance. They heralded the proximity of the dragon's cave, and I was not feeling at all prepared for another descent into those fearsome regions.

"Don't strain yourself, but never mind them," the Prior said of my difficulties. "Think about them as little as possible. Just keep to whatever you feel in your heart is the best way to commune with the Holy Spirit. Do it every day, never neglect it. Don't fret. Everything works itself out in the end." He is a real Bodhisattva, a Christian-Buddhist Bodhisattva, I thought.

The last evening of this visit was spent in Cambridge, where the Prior was invited to dinner with a few of the members of the Cambridge Buddhist Association. One of the members, a gifted young pianist, introduced himself to the Prior while the latter was standing under an enormous fiddle-leaf fig, a tree that had been purchased in a local shopping center and cultivated to a height of eleven feet over the years. The branches had spread about to embrace part of the room, and one or two branches had started to grow down from the ceiling.

"An extraordinary vegetation!" said the Prior.

"Somebody came the other day who asked if it was one of those famous man-eating plants," I remarked.

"And," said the young member of the Buddhist Association with mock solemnity, "of course you told him that it only eats Christians!"

The dinner was a success, and the Prior had a long and fruitful talk with one of our senior members, Olga Averino, a singer who was born in Czarist Russia. A goddaughter of Tchaikovsky and a soloist for the Boston Symphony Orchestra while it was under the direction of Serge Koussevitzky, this wise and distinguished lady had discovered the value of concentrated spiritual practice and meditation during the course of a life filled with challenging and often disrupting adventures while an émigré in China and the United States.

"When all dissolves in chaos around and on top of you, it is important to know what is the absolute and eternal, to know it just from your own experience. No abstract philosophy or dogma can help you when there is evil and destruction all about you." The Prior was much moved by the lady's warmth, her humor, and her humanity. "She must have lived and suffered a lot; one can tell it from her wisdom and compassion," he said.

I returned the Prior to his monastery the following morning. In the car we became involved in a lively discussion of religious art; and somehow the discussion turned to a matter that we were to take up again and again, the Buddha nature of all beings and the "hierarchy of being" of the Prior's Christianity. In mid-discussion, I suddenly noticed the gas pedal was not responding. An empty gas tank! I pulled the car onto a parking strip at the edge of the highway and we quickly got out of the car and climbed the steep grassy bank above the road. It was hot and humid. The Prior, I thought miserably, must be dreadfully uncomfortable in his hot black clerical suit. We sat together in the tall grass and the Prior mopped his steaming face with his handkerchief.

"If parents of one of the students in the priory school should happen to pass by and see me here with a glamor girl, what'll that do for my image!" he said, wiping perspiration from his face. I was too hot to look at all glamorous, but I felt very contrite, the more so because he was not in the least cross in spite of his obvious discomfort. Fortunately, after about ten minutes a taxi stopped and the driver was persuaded to buy us a can of gas. We were on our way again, hot but unharmed, within about half an hour. By then the drift of our conversation had changed. Nevertheless, in a letter that the Prior wrote a day or so after his return to the priory, Christian iconography and the question of sentient nonhuman beings came up again.

4 August 1964

Dear Elsie:
Now I am back in my monastery with the pleasantest

memories of my visit with you in Milton, on the Cape and in Cambridge; and no time at the moment to tell you how much I enjoyed it all and appreciated your care.

It is generally admitted, I think, that Christian iconography, especially the modern (or post-Renaissance) Western variety, is not nearly as pleasing to the eye as the Buddhist. The kind of pictorial realism you deplore I deplore too. But shouldn't one be more tolerant? After all, there are degrees of understanding and I think becoming a "superior person" is much to be discouraged. In any case "per Christum hominem ad Christum deum" is a Catholic axiom: "through the wounds of humanity to the light of divinity." Doesn't that make some sense? All the more so as the average Catholic doesn't aim to be "enlightened". He is just struggling along and often needs some props that others can dispense with. Besides, as Pope Paul has just pointed out in his first encyclical, the church has still a lot to learn about itself.

Perhaps one of the things to be learned is a greater sensitiveness to other forms of life. Though my own guess is that if one has due compassion for the *human* animal in all its variety of forms, one will show due respect and affection towards other species of life. Besides, as I tried to argue in our talks, there is a hierarchy of values in this matter which should not be overlooked.

You do not trust yourself as much as you should. According to Zen Catholicism to trust your True Self is to trust God. And you have a strong and enlightening True Self. So you must not kid me, in a charming and playful feline way, with any professions of mock modesty. Nor must you allow any superstition into religion. Devotion and adoration to what is adorable; but no superstition with its suggestions of magic. Am I being too tough and logical? But you are worthy of it. Remember the words of the Buddha to Ananda: "Be a light unto yourself." So be calm and at peace and sit quietly.

Devotedly,
Your Zen Catholic Prior

Buddhists feel fellowship with all living things that experience pain and death, even as do humans themselves: stories abound in the Jatakas, as well as in Buddhist scriptures, of animals, two-legged and four-, feeling and practicing compassion for one another. In Mahayana teaching, man is inextricably related to all other beings on his planet, to all forms of life and sublife. Ecology may be novel for Christians, but Mahayana Buddhists have always been ecologically aware. Before the advent of Christianity, Buddhist sovereigns planted shade trees and created watering places for man and beast alike when they wished to undertake meritorious religious projects. "Is it possible to imagine a landscape without a man?" inquires an old Chinese proverb, and continues: "Or a man without a landscape?" Japanese and Chinese Buddhists have always believed that even the ground on which man stands he should respect, not misuse, if he is to survive and fulfill his human potential and his destiny.

It seemed to me that my Prior represented an institution and a philosophy that was overzealous in its mistaken desire to separate man from the rest of creation. Greek-inspired Christian philosophy had developed an inflated Manichaean entity called a soul, able to soar into the clouds far above the "brittle clay." My conversations and correspondence with the Zen Catholic Prior returned to this subject over and over, though not always on a very lofty plane. For example: the Catholic magazine that I read in my efforts to understand Catholicism published an article with references to Catholic saints who had befriended species other than their own. One example given was Saint Benedict Joseph Labre, who allowed fleas to settle on his arms to make a meal off him.

I inquired of the Prior if he approved of this example of saint-hood. He replied that "Saint B. J. Labre's attachment to fleas was not because he looked forward to their spiritual realization (the evolution of their Buddha nature!) but because he wanted them to bite him and so add a few jewels to his crown of glory!" This, I thought to myself, was typical of the Christian approach to the rest of creation, indeed to the cosmos itself. Man was be-lieved to be the center of all things, for whom fleas and mountains and stars were created. Was it surprising that so many Christians and post-Christians felt lost in a cold, threatening universe, when their religion appeared to teach them that it was a vast warehouse created by a Supertechnician expressly for their physical com-fort and as a limitless source of materials and possibilities to aid their efforts toward self-glorification? The power and the glory forever and ever?

I sent for some literature from an organization called the National Catholic Society for Animal Welfare and passed it on to the Prior, along with a pamphlet circulated by an organiza-tion called World Wildlife, dedicated to the preservation of animal species that humanity might soon crowd off the planet completely. The Prior replied: "So we're back again with our dumb friends! I think the Buddhist Reverend Mother tends to become rather obsessed about a too restricted section of sentient beings. Does not her compassion and benevolence need to con-cern itself a little more with the suffering and ignorant members of her own species? Cats and dogs and birds and caterpillars all have their place, but shouldn't one be a little more concerned about the 'still sad music of humanity' etc.?"

My practical and always down-to-earth husband read the fore-going and said he thought the shrill discordant music of too much humanity was the really relevant matter to which both Buddhists and Christians should be applying themselves. Then he fished through his desk and came up with an article from a population-control organization, in which it was observed that in a not too distant future human beings would have two choices of food, both drab: plankton and other people.

"Send your Prior that!" he said. Somehow I didn't think it would be received with much enthusiasm or even interest. The priory was surrounded by flourishing farm country and by fields in which grazed some perfectly edible cows—edible, that is, from his Christian point of view. I could not help thinking of the little Londoners sent out into the English countryside to escape the bombs of World War II. They were horrified to discover that country milk was procured from cows. The only milk they had ever known grew in bottles.

The Prior had one very Buddhist area of awareness: he did not like cut flowers. Buddhists in Japan have always cut a few flowers for their arrangements, but masses of cut flowers in vases are rare on Buddhist altars. Flowers, bushes, and trees were never needlessly destroyed or injured until around the end of the Meiji era (1868–1912), I was told by my Japanese-British friend Captain Jack Brinkley.

"One thing," wrote the Prior in a letter. "I regard plants as sentient beings too, and think cut flowers rather like dead animals in dissecting rooms. According to Zen Catholic metaphysics, dead (i.e., cut) flowers cannot 'long' to praise the Buddha. They praise him best when they are—like all other sentient beings, especially humans—alive and flourishing, that is, being their true selves. Therefore, flowers for ceremonial purposes should be embedded in plant pots, and so alive—that is, if those higher up in the hierarchy of being insist (as they have the right to do) on having flowers to adorn the altars and shrines in their churches and pagodas."

"I think it is all very nice and very true what you say about the flowers," I said to the Prior when next we met. "But if you think flowers should be allowed to live and blossom unimpeded, how about those poor cats whom your colleague Father So-and-So practices his marksmanship on?" Apparently this reverend inhabitant of the priory was a great amateur marksman and proud of his skill in bagging cats and other small sentient creatures who were unfortunate enough to roam the monastic premises.

"He has a gun club," said the Prior.

"And you can't stop him?" I exclaimed.

"A prior can only try to reason with people; he has no real control over their activities."

"And if a monk decides to set up on the priory premises some houses of prostitution, a little 'flower town' as it used to be called in Japan, is that all right, too?"

"Surely some people would be captivated, but, of course, if such activity was brought to my attention, I might have to attend to it."

"But gun-toting monks in a country not at war! One of the current members of the Buddhist Association comes from the far north of New England, where people are poor and everyone hunts, partly for food and partly for amusement. Our friend's father was killed in a hunting accident, as was another member of his family, who was shot by his teen-age son. Every year in his state people shoot each other, not infrequently members of their own family, their own children, their own parents. Does it stop them from hunting? No, they're at it again as soon as the season rolls round! He says they really enjoy killing; it's a blood lust, a primitive variety of sexual pleasure. They can't control it. But they are lay people, and they aren't prattling on about 'Good News' and 'Kingdom of God.' They aren't pretending to set any kind of an example for anyone. They are poor and frustrated. Killing is a compensation for all the frustrations in their lives. It is not hard to understand why such people enjoy the pursuit of smaller or weaker creatures in order to torment and kill, not even hard to understand why some of them get around to shooting up an occasional relative, either!"

"Oh, lots of people might enjoy just such an opportunity," said the Prior. I decided to try another tack.

"Your English bobbies go about in all kinds of dangerous places, trusting only in God and a night stick; they have no guns and people respect and admire them for it."

"That," said the Prior, "is another story. That is England." The Prior always had the last word, which of course was the right and privilege of a reverend and venerable roshi, Buddhist or Christian.

The following October the Cambridge Buddhist Association received a visit from the Venerable Shunryu Suzuki. Suzuki Roshi was in charge of a Buddhist temple, as well as a Zen center for Westerners, in San Francisco. He had been living in the United States for about six years and had learned English and gathered together a large group of people seriously interested in meditation. I had met him in San Francisco after one of my journeys to Japan and been greatly impressed with his integrity, his goodness, and particularly his willingness to work out ways of traditional Buddhist practice really suitable for contemporary Westerners. He wrote that he would be arriving on a Wednesday night, and we planned to meet him at the airport.

Tuesday afternoon we returned to Cambridge from Cape Cod, and several of us set to work housecleaning. That evening the library cum meditation room was in the process of being scrubbed down when the doorbell rang. My husband climbed down a ladder and opened the front door. Suzuki Roshi was on the doorstep with a smile on his face. He was amused to find us amid preparations for his arrival. In spite of our protests, he immediately tied back his long kimono sleeves and insisted on joining in "all these preparations for the important day of my coming." The following morning, after breakfast and a meditation session, and after I had left the house for shopping, he found himself a tall ladder, sponges, and pails. He then set to work scrubbing

Cambridge grease, grime, and general pollution from the outside of the windows in the meditation room. When I returned with the groceries, I discovered him on the ladder, polishing with such undivided attention that he did not even hear my approach. He had removed his black silk kimono and was dressed only in his Japanese union suit. This is quite acceptable attire in Japan. Nevertheless, I could not help wondering how the sedate Cambridge ladies in the adjoining apartment house would react to the sight of a shaven-headed man in long underwear at work just outside their windows.

The roshi loved his first visit to Cape Cod when we took him there for a weekend. Early each morning he sat on a large rock on the beach and chanted his sutras. He was delighted with our rock garden and set about weeding and trimming our bushes with enthusiasm and skill. He made himself a miniature garden inside a large mussel shell with moss, berries, and a little sand. He said that he wanted to take a bit of New England back to California with him.

Before the roshi left, I asked him if he thought it possible for a person to be both Buddhist and Christian. "Well," he said, "I know very little about Christianity, and I have always thought the best thing about it is some of the music. The great music, that is, not what you hear in ordinary churches. Some Christians, some Christian ministers come to Zen Center, but I don't think they can become Buddhists." Later he remarked that the people he had observed wandering through one religion after another didn't seem to be able to find any peace or understanding. "But," he said, "maybe there are some individuals who can do it." I explained to him that New England had no Japanese or other traditional community where Buddhism could develop naturally and organically as in California or Hawaii. I told him that quite a few people would surely practice meditation, but possibly not as Buddhists. Then I read to him a few quotations from *Zen Catholicism*.

"Of course," he said, "from one point of view, perhaps even the most important one, a label such as Christian or Buddhist has no meaning. However, actually there is Buddhism and there is Christianity; they are both living traditions, living communities." Then he asked me: "Could you become a Christian? To me it does not seem that it would be possible. You do not seem to me like any Christian I have ever known. You seem to live quite naturally in the Buddhist manner, with the Buddhist, especially Japanese Buddhist, feeling about all nature, about the Great Nature."

"I agree," I replied, "about the labels, but also there seem to me to be certain aspects of a Westerner's psychic experience, mostly intangible, that are tied up in Christianity. The Western Buddhists I know who really seem to live their Buddhism often find that they can read some Christian mystics and feel close to them in a way that was not possible before they became Buddhists. For example, Mother Juliana of Norwich or the book *The Cloud of Unknowing* holds considerable interest for some Western Buddhists. As for me, except for *The Cloud of Unknowing, Zen Catholicism*, and some of the books of Thomas Merton, I cannot usually read about Christianity with much benefit. However, I can feel a sense of transcendence, I suppose it is, in a contemplatively sung or even spoken Mass. There is something very strong and profound if one makes an 'empty' mind during this ritual; and while I am participating I forget all about Buddhism or Christianity or anything except a kind of communion, a communion with all creation. Then afterwards, of course, I cannot help remembering that Christians, influenced by centuries of Platonism, do not understand how much all manifestations of creation need and depend on one another. It seems to me that Christian orthodoxy has created a sort of fetish out of humanity. A fetish and a leviathan. No sacrifice, no destruction or slaughter is too great if it is done in the name of humanity, if it leads to the 'glorification' of man or what one theologian calls the 'hominization' of the world. That is what I cannot accept in Christianity. However, when one takes part in the Mass *mushin,* egolessly, such intellectual problems do not arise."

"Well," said Roshi, "there must be many things in the spirit of man and it is impossible, maybe, for one person to understand them all. But you have the Tokudo of a wonderful teacher, you are living and practicing in a Buddhist way. Some questions are interesting theoretically, but they have no sure answers and one may do harm to oneself and even to others if one puts too much or the wrong kind of attention on them. Just remember your Buddha nature, my Buddha nature, the Prior's Buddha nature, and the Buddha nature in all people, in the dogs and cats and other beings everywhere. That's what is really important."

The Western insight set in the tradition of the East—, I thought and wondered if, in a shrinking world, East and West would long retain much meaning. Now it is possible to travel eastward rapidly enough to land in the West more quickly than if one proceeded by a slower conveyance in a westerly direction in the first place. Presently Buddhism and Christianity seem like two separate vessels with sails set for separate ports, if one approaches them intellectually, socially, or institutionally. But all institutions are in the throes of change: tomorrow's Buddhism, tomorrow's Christianity could well be seen as clearly headed for the same destination, though leaving port in separate directions.

I wrote a description of these conversations with Suzuki Roshi to the Prior, who was out of the country for some weeks. He replied: "Your recent guest, Suzuki Roshi, appears to be rather a wise and wonderful person and I feel that under his guidance you are in good hands." On the subject of being a Catholic or Buddhist, he added: "One of my private little 'heresies' is that people are often not improved but rather 'disimproved' by becoming card-carrying Roman Catholics. The 'naturals' for conversion are emotionally disturbed youngsters, who are obviously meant to flop into the arms of 'Sancta Mater Ecclesia,' or liturgically minded laymen (or Anglican parsons) who won't be happy until they are ecclesiastically 'with it.' Now and again there is someone like Newman, who was a true seeker, but my observation is that it is for other reasons besides the truth of things that many people become Catholics.

"That is why I'm not particularly happy about this 'Ecumenism.' I don't see it amounting to much more than a sincere effort at ecclesiastical togetherness with the view to forming a common front against contemporary 'Godlessness' (whatever precisely that is)."

The Prior gave many retreats to Catholic nuns, most of whom surely appreciated his talks and counsel. Once he wrote from Canada: "I have just finished talking for three-quarters of an hour to 200 nuns, most of them dears. Though one of them greeted me with the remark: 'I have been looking forward eagerly to your retreat,' to which I replied, 'I hope you won't be disappointed.' She responded, 'No, I have prayed'!"

It wasn't always possible for outsiders to understand the rationale of Christian prayer, I decided. However, the way of prayer favored by the Prior, "Thy will be done"—"without," as he so aptly added, "trying to form a nice heartwarming, emotionally satisfying little image of who the Thy is"—was really a Christian mantra, which was quite consistent with the spirit of Buddhism. On the subject of prayer, the Prior wrote: "I cannot get unduly excited about intercessory prayer in any shape or form. Everything is in God's good hands, so why plague Him unduly with one's own notions about what He should do. All our petty little requests have as their first premise, 'Thy will be done,' so let's not bother the good Lord too much about particularities."

In 1965 the Prior visited us once or twice in Cambridge, and each morning he took part in Buddhist meditation. He appeared to appreciate these sessions rather more than the young Japanese girl who was living with us at the time. This young lady had been sent to us by a Buddhist priest living in California so that she could have a taste of American life outside a Japanese family. In order to improve her English, our Japanese visitor watched late-night movies on television and rarely went to sleep until after two o'clock in the morning. Needless to say, she was very groggy when our zazen sessions started at 7:30. One morning at breakfast the Prior asked her if she liked to do zazen. She replied with disarming frankness, "I hate zazen. But I am a Buddhist; my family is very traditional, so I have to follow the customs in this Buddhist household."

Early in 1965, the Prior decided to experiment with a group of schoolboys in his priory to see how short sessions of "Catholic zazen" might work. The experiment seemed to prove a success, and at least one schoolboy after graduation wrote the Prior to say that his spiritual life was greatly deepened and strengthened by the experience. About this Catholic zazen, the Prior wrote: "I am inclined to think that Catholic zazen might turn out to be more peaceful and relaxed than the original Buddhist variety. I think the Christian emphasis is that we should be less effortful, leave more to the Self (equals God) one can't control. Therefore it seems to me, and I am sure that this only expresses your own thoughts, one shouldn't expect any quick results in terms of consciousness. 'Ripeness is all,' says Shakespeare. Shouldn't it develop slowly throughout a lifetime?"

"Ripeness is all"—this is certainly an important Zen principle, a central consideration in all Mahayana Buddhism. But the Zen masters also maintain: "The greater the doubt, the greater the enlightenment," which is only to say that the *mu ke ge* (no effort is necessary) of which the Heart Sutra speaks is a discovery made only with the knowledge of the insufficiency of one's very best efforts to achieve enlightenment. Then only is it possible really to know the important truth of the koan that the means is the end and that ends and means cannot be separated. I wrote something along those lines in reply to the Prior's letter.

One of the Prior's Catholic zazen students inquired how Buddhists define "religion." The Christian definition, he observed, is dependence on a Supreme Being. The Prior asked how I would go about answering the question. I replied that not all Buddhists would agree on an answer, but possibly Theravada Buddhists would say "dependence on a Supreme Law" (the Dhamma), whereas most Mahayana Buddhists might prefer "realization of our Buddha nature." However, it seemed to me that being, law, and nature were all conceptualizations with a rather limited capacity for conveying what was actually in the minds and spirits of those who used them. With this the Prior agreed.

All things considered, we had managed, after about a year of talks, correspondence, and meditation together, to understand each other extraordinarily well. I felt much gratitude to the Zen Catholic Roshi, shortened to Z.C.R., as I finally began to call him. He had the great gift of knowing how to teach without teaching. Moreover, I felt that he had deepened my understanding of that essential "emptiness" necessary for true friendship and for compassion. One can be neither Buddhist nor Christian without the beginnings of such an understanding. To know oneself is to forget one's self, and to forget one's self is to make enlightenment possible. And why not a Buddhist disciple for a Zen Catholic Roshi in a changing, agitated world, where geographical and cultural boundaries are dissolving all around us! Sectarian spirits, Buddhist and Christian, would not find such an arrangement either acceptable or comprehensible. For some, labels and boundaries are of primary importance. Once the Z.C.R. wrote: "I am very glad to hear that you have spiritually outgrown such books as: 'Why I Became a Catholic'! However, you might write one on 'Why I Have a Z.C.R.'! This would really be interesting."

14 THE DEATH MASK

Dreams, delusions, flowers of air—
why should we be so anxious to have them
in our grasp?

Hsinhsinming

A FEW WEEKS BEFORE one of my Japanese sojourns I was introduced to a very interesting woman, a poet and musicologist, who had practiced Zen meditation under the able direction of one of the first Japanese monks to take up residence in America. After ten years of practice her teacher had died, and she had been converted to the Greek Orthodox church.

We had tea together in her Beacon Hill apartment.

"Look," said the lady after we had talked for a bit, "there is something I am disturbed about, something in my possession that I don't know what to do with." From a large box carefully wrapped in an old shawl she produced a plaster cast of a fine strong face with eyes closed as in sleep.

"The death mask of my teacher, made only about an hour or so after his death," she said. "And really I am at a loss as to what to do with it. I loved and respected Osho [teacher]; we all did. Now, however, thanks to his teaching, I have been able to return to Christianity and I have no more contact with Buddhism or Buddhists. My present friends and associates know nothing about that period in my life. I would not discuss it with them, as I know there is nothing in their experience or education which would enable them to understand it." Then she produced a box containing a Buddhist rosary and one or two other artifacts that indicated participation in a Buddhist initiation.

"What do they mean?" she reflected thoughtfully. "I wonder what exactly these things mean," and she handed me the rosary to look at. "We never asked Osho questions like that. Of course, we realized the ceremony involved our relationship to him and to the group, but the exact significance of the ritual Osho did not explain." Together we looked at her sleeping teacher's countenance. It was a good face and the expression was peaceful; there was no aura of death about it. But his disciple obviously had not been able to harmonize the spirit of that teacher and loyalty to his memory with what she felt to be the requirements of her current situation.

"Maybe," I said uncertainly, "you could burn everything." Recently Shimpu had shown me a Christian missionary pamphlet containing a photograph of a Japanese family throwing their Buddhist altar and rosaries into a large bonfire in their garden. I couldn't help remembering their wooden smiles and Shimpu's disgust at what he considered a tasteless and repelling performance. To soothe him I said, "Perhaps we should buy some Bibles and make a little fire in my garden—and you could take lots of photographs—"

"Yes, maybe," and he laughed. "Well, after all, it is a rather funny idea, I suppose."

I said I thought it would be funny if Buddhists did it, at least publicly.

I never learned what the lady actually did with the death

mask. Sometimes I wondered about it. Nevertheless, it was obvious to me that she had learned something during the ten years with her teacher, her Osho. She was gentle, forthright, and open, without a trace of self-righteousness, smugness, or bigotry. Surely it was not important whatever she finally decided to do with those mementos of her formal association with the Buddhist tradition. Her teacher's strong, wise spirit was very much aware and living in the sensibilities and personality of his former disciple. This was something no fire, no ritual or new allegiance could possibly change or affect.

In an autobiographical poem on the spiritual life, this lady wrote some lines that expressed, in a Western way, one aspect of her zazen experience:

> "For man's awareness has
> an orbic sheath.
> All 'round about us flows
> an ocean mood;
> Clouds of unknowing,
> wisdom's greater part,
> assist us, nourish, comfort and sustain."*

I described the foregoing to my Zen Catholic Roshi in one of my letters to him, and he replied:

1 March 1965

My dearest D.R.M. [Disciple and Reverend Mother]:

Thank you for your long and interesting letter which has just arrived.

First, what needs to be considered is that we are both helped and hindered by emotional attachment to the *cultus*, whether Buddhist or Catholic. We are helped in as much as it gives a focus to religious concern, and also some consola-

*Unpublished poem by Mariquita Platov, author of *A Christmas Candle* and *Tease the Tiger's Nose*.

tion, burdened insofar as the intuitive and penetrative mind is not going to rest until it gets beyond the cultus. But you can't and are not meant to get beyond the cultus by any kind of personal effort. This is the passage from Bhakti to Gnosis or Sophia. Not that the Gnosis-Sophia state eliminates Bhakti, it merely treats it with detachment, rather humorously.

As for me, I am spending odd moments with the philosopher Wittgenstein, who has long fascinated me. He strikes me—as he has others—as a very Zennist spirit. 'Don't think but look,' he kept repeating to his students. And then that wonderful saying: 'If we take eternity to mean not infinite temporal duration but timelessness, then eternal life belongs to those who live in the present.'

I am also reading with delight and immense benefit *The Tiger's Cave*. What a wonderful book! How significant is the notion of life being a tightrope walked between two cliffs, below being upturned sword blades. On the tightrope of life one performs stunts—the abbot's stunt being that of a Zen—, mine that of a Benedictine—, monk. All that appeals to me immensely as does the whole personality of the writer.

Wednesday is the Christian beginning of Lent and Ash Wednesday: but it is also March 3 and the Feast of my patron saint. So you may appropriately say a little prayer for this two-legged sentient being to Amida Buddha, whose image presides over me (from the top shelf!) as I write this.

You are very dear to God and to many sentient beings, so be of good heart. May I keep *The Tiger's Cave* for awhile?

Devotedly,
Your Z.C.R.

15 PREPARATIONS FOR A JOURNEY

It never leaves this place and is always perfect.
When you look for it, you find you can't see it.
You can't get at it, you can't be rid of it.
When you do neither, there it is!
When you are silent, it speaks;
When you speak it is silent.

Chengtaoke

IN THE SPRING of 1967 the Prior told us that he definitely wished to make a journey to Asia after his retirement from the priory that same summer. He wanted to return to his native England ("the rock from which I was hewn") by way of India and Japan.

"Won't you and Jack meet me in Tokyo?" he asked. "Maybe you would be able to introduce me to some of your interesting Buddhist friends there. You have told me so much about them and I would like to have an opportunity to be face to face with them myself!"

Unfortunately, the well-known Zen scholar Dr. Daisetz Suzuki had died the summer before. I had known Dr. Suzuki from his six-month stay in Cambridge in 1957 and had hoped to have him and the Prior meet. Captain Jack Brinkley, my Japanese-British friend, had also died. However, the name of a young Japanese woman, quite an old friend, who had practiced Zen Buddhist meditation for more than ten years in Kyoto came to mind. She was an excellent interpreter and guide, who I thought would be able to take the Prior to visit some non-English-speaking Buddhist personalities. Once she had brought to America a group of elderly and non-English-speaking Shinto priests, and on other occasions she had accompanied a Buddhist abbot on his lecture tours. She had got her charges on and off buses, in and out of hotels and museums, and finally safely back to their own country.

"Can you imagine, Elsie," she said. "The first time I took all those old Shinto priests to a restaurant, when the bill was brought they all started to undress themselves! I really got a shock. They were wearing large, old-fashioned money belts concealed under their clothing."

America the dangerous! Could one blame an elderly foreign tourist in America for taking every possible precaution? Anyone who has ever watched the news reports from the United States over European or Asian television knows that the United States presents an alarming image of volatile violence and madness, adventure in the unexpected, to the inhabitants of the outside world. One young German girl who planned a visit of some months in our home in 1968 wrote to me shortly before her departure for the States: "When do you expect the revolution to begin? My parents are terribly upset about my visit to America, and my mother has been crying. Is it really safe for me to come to your country?"

My Japanese friend, an experienced guide for Buddhist as well as Shinto priests, was delighted to have an opportunity to take a "Catholic father" around her country. She felt that here was a promising possibility to learn about Western spirituality and monasticism firsthand. Together we arranged an itinerary that a year or so later tentatively was to have been followed by the late Thomas Merton. It included visits to urban monasteries and country temples. The visits were arranged as informal meetings, with opportunities for long, relaxed conversations. The Zen Catholic Roshi was not interested in only an academic exchange of dogma and formulae.

"Four or five years ago," I wrote to my friend in Japan, "I could not have imagined myself arranging such a journey for a Christian cleric. I have never been interested in what is vaguely called 'comparative religion' and I think much of what is called dialogue is simply an exchange of monologues, a *mizukakeron,* that is, each person so busy watering his own rice field that he cannot see beyond it. Nevertheless, this Prior is an interesting person, an open-minded and, it seems to me, enlightened Christian. This is an era of talk and change, change and talk. I guess we must all accommodate ourselves!"

Mrs. Ruth Fuller Sasaki, the first American woman to become a resident temple priest, or *jushoku,* in Japan was consulted about where the Prior should stay during his Japanese visit. She suggested International House in Tokyo and the Japanese inn attached to a Western-style hotel in Kyoto. As things eventually worked themselves out, these were the places where he resided during most of his stay in Japan.

A young friend of the Prior, Harold Talbott, eager to see the Far East for the first time, was invited to act as the Prior's temporary secretary. In his teens Harold had been converted to Catholicism; but he was also a serious student of Buddhism and had studied Sanskrit at Harvard. He was particularly enthusiastic about the Prior's plan to meet the Dalai Lama in Dharmsala, as even then his karma was drawing him toward the Tibetan tradition. After his year of pilgrimage in the company of the Prior, he was to return alone to India and to devote himself to years of study with Tibetan teachers.

Before their departure for Asia by way of Hawaii, the Zen Catholic Roshi decided that he should spend several months reading and meditating on the forthcoming journey. He planned to stay with us on Cape Cod for some weeks, after which he was to spend about a month in an Episcopalian household in California. The Episcopalian hostess-to-be had a beautiful ranch and was famous for her generosity and warmhearted hospitality.

Our household is not a conventional American home, nor are we exactly an American sort of family. Over the years our "family" has consisted of Japanese graduate students and professors, as well as a succession of German, Swiss, and Japanese "house-daughters," *Haustöchter* as the Germans used to call them. Two married couples, both Japanese, stayed with us, one of the couples for six months and the other for nearly two years, the wife returning to Japan before her husband so that her baby could be born in her native country. One Japanese girl who spent about three months with us at the request of a California Buddhist priest, after a month or so in the house, informed us that she knew all about "usual American life from both the Japanese and American television," and "here is not America at all."

One evening, shortly before the Prior's arrival, we were having dinner with two of our housedaughters: a Japanese graduate student, Misato Toda, at Boston University under the sponsorship of the Cambridge Buddhist Association, and a young German girl who had been introduced to us by my husband's parents in Switzerland.

"I have just written to my mother," said Misato, "and told her that I am living in a typically European household, though this is America, and that I am eating wonderful European food!"

"Oh," cried Bärbel from Germany, "the first time I wrote to

my mother from this country I told her that I was living in a typical Japanese household and learning Japanese cooking. In fact, I sent her your recipe for tempura!"

The Z.C.R. liked only what he called "plain cooking," he informed us on his arrival for the prejourney visit.

"What is plain cooking?" asked Misato and Bärbel with one voice. The Prior thought a moment, then he said: "Meat and peas, with possibly a touch of cauliflower. And none of Elsie's salads or pink lemonade, no tomatoes. No mustard, please! Mustard creates an irascible nature!"

Misato made him some green tea, which he drank politely but without enthusiasm. When he had finished, he asked if he might have another cup, this time of real tea, as "that wet green powder" had made him very thirsty.

"No, grandfather," said Misato firmly. Misato had decided she should have him for a grandfather after a minor altercation during a lively discussion on the relationship of Buddhism and history that had taken place after a zazen meeting. Misato, like all spirited though traditional Japanese girls, knew just how to deal with grandfathers who needed to be briefed on the current state of the world.

"In Japan," she said severely, "you will be obliged to drink a lot of green tea in temples, and it is important for you to appear to like it." She provided two more cups of tea made of "wet green powder," and he drank them with remarkable docility.

"I love grandfather!" exclaimed Misato. "I understand him very well. He is like a traditional Japanese man! In one moment he is the Almighty Emperor and we cannot say anything at all to him, just carry out his wishes. In the next minute he is like a sweet child and he will do just whatever I tell him."

"Grandfather" struggled gamely with chopsticks and tried a little of each of the Japanese delicacies that Misato provided for him. "If the meat is always presented in such small morsels," he said, "I shall surely starve or have no time for learning about Buddhism while I am in Japan!"

"Never mind," said Misato. "In Japanese cities you can always find a Western-style restaurant that will be pleased to give you a steak completely equipped with knife and fork." Misato was a very Westernized Japanese girl, who preferred a Western diet, washed down with large quantities of Japanese tea.

"You will surely go to Hell!" Ingrid, one of the German inhabitants of our household, told her severely one day.

"Whatever for?" asked Misato, puzzled.

"You eat meat nearly every day, even large steaks. Buddhists must not eat dead animals," said Ingrid firmly. Ingrid had decided to brave the revolution after all, despite her mother's tears, and to spend some time in our household. She is a faithful and devout Roman Catholic.

"But," protested Misato, "meat is a kind of medicine and Buddhists may have all kinds of medicines for their health! Living in America is rather exhausting for me and I must make myself strong with steaks."

"What is *Bodaishin?* How do you think of the Buddha nature?" the Zen Catholic Prior asked Misato one afternoon as they drank Japanese tea together.

"It is what is best and deepest inside of us, what enlightens us even if we don't know how or why. All the time it is working inside of us even though we cannot be conscious of it. It works outside of us too: in you, in everyone—though really it cannot be properly described by either inside or outside."

"Is it like a Christian soul?"

"Maybe. Except I don't know what is that Christian soul. Bodaishin is everywhere, in all beings and everything to some degree or other. Maybe only potential, awaiting long evolution."

"In the animals, like this overindulged and underdisciplined cat?" and he pointed to the feline member of our family, who was sitting on his knees.

"Of course." Then Misato inquired, "Isn't there also a Christ nature which develops inside the Christian people? Is it like the Buddha nature, always there, or is it, so to say, injected at the time when Christians participate in baptism?"

"Actually," said the Zen Catholic Roshi, "one of the sayings of Jesus is that the kingdom of God is within you and 'where two or three are gathered together in my name, there am I in the midst of you.' There is the True Self in each of us, the True Self which waits and prays for enlightenment by grace, by the Holy Spirit. For Christians this means living according to God's will and not inspired by one's own ego, that is, in the spirit of Christ. Baptism, however, is a gift of the Spirit, a gift of God."

"Maybe I can understand that," said Misato. "It seems beautiful."

In order to look into many aspects of Asian Buddhism, to see the tradition "in its own setting," the Zen Catholic Roshi departed for Japan, Thailand, and India a month or so later. On his way to Japan he stopped for a few days in Hawaii, where we had arranged for him to stay with our friends the Aitkens in Honolulu.

Bob Aitken had first become interested in Zen during World War II, when he was taken prisoner of war off Wake Island and was interned in a prison camp in Osaka. A fellow prisoner was the well-known English Zen scholar R. H. Blyth, and the two became fast friends. This friendship was to decide the whole future course of Bob's life. As this is being written, he and his wife are living on the Hawaiian island of Maui. They are in charge of three Zen communities: one on the island of Maui, a second on Kauai, and a third in Honolulu. The young people living in these three sanghas are seeking a new way of communion with one another, as well as with our abused and neglected home, the earth. They spend their days working at carpentry and gardening. They also take part in traditional zazen and Buddhist chanting.

Shortly after the Prior arrived in Hawaii, he wrote me the following letter from the Aitkens' home:

14–15 August 1967

My dearest D.R.M.:

I sent you and Jack a meager postcard just before having the Aitkens to lunch at the hotel—and then being transported by them to their beautiful home and zendo, meditation hall. Both Harold and I are very happy here during our all too brief stay. Bob and Ann seem to us, and a great many others hereabouts, quite wonderful people, and they appear to like having us here. At supper yesterday Bob gave us a wonderful disquisition on haiku poetry. And Ann in all sorts of ways is being most patient, compassionate and helpful: driving us around and acting as chauffeur and guide in semitropical heat.

On Sunday evening we took part in the meditation, the zazen session in the Aitkens' home. All very impressive, with lots of gongs, bells, wooden clappers, applications of the big stick (I forget the technical name) and chanting of sutras. After the ceremony Bob gave a nice introduction to your Z.C.R. and his secretary—there were about ten members present—and invited me to sit in the center of things and hold forth. I just threw out a few thoughts on traditional Christianity and its need for an infusion of new light. This sparked a general discussion and question period, to which Bob made some very wise and relevant contributions.

As you doubtless know, it will be eight years this October since this Buddhist group was founded. I imagine that the Aitkens have struggled and suffered for so worthwhile an enterprise. My observation is that they attract remarkable personalities. For instance, on Sunday night, there was present a nineteen-year-old girl who is studying anthropology, in which she has majored at the University of Hawaii. She asked me all sorts of questions about Paul Tillich. She works several hours a day in a Honolulu bar which she is to leave in a few weeks for Japan, traveling third class by boat. Eventually she plans to reach Saigon, where she wants to work in an orphanage to help children whose parents have been killed by American bombs. Another girl, a Hawaiian third-generation Japanese named Diana, has just graduated from Barnard College in New York City, majoring in mathematics and philosophy. She and Harold (who is proving quite indispensable: e.g., he is packing our bags while I am writing this) got along together conspicuously well, and she told him of her plans for herself. She intends to give up her job in a local computer firm, to go and live by herself in a little shack in the hills and spend most of her time in meditation!

Now we must make for the airport, and thence Tokyo. When next you write the Aitkens I'm sure you will tell them how deeply appreciative and touched I am by the hospitality shown us here. There seems to have been such a meeting of minds and hearts.

I shall look forward to hearing from you in Tokyo. Till then—God bless you.

Your devoted
Z.C.R.

The fruits of the Zen Catholic Prior's journey, his "Larger Ecumenism," appeared in the autumn of 1968 in a book entitled *Conversations: Christian and Buddhist. Encounters in Japan,** a wise and mellow book for Christians who have realized the importance of "not playing God but letting God play," and for Buddhists who

---

*Dom Aelred Graham, *Conversations: Christian and Buddhist. Encounters in Japan* (New York, Harcourt Brace Jovanovich, 1968).

can recognize and appreciate a true "man of no rank." The Prior's informal discussions with Japanese monks and teachers, as well as with a few English and American expatriates living in Japan while studying Buddhist philosophy and meditation, began with a visit to Misato's Zen teacher in Tokyo. It also included a sojourn with Rindo Fujimoto, my Buddhist roshi, in his country temple, and discussions with other monks and lay people whom I had met on my travels some years earlier, friends with whom I still corresponded. These friendly, open-hearted people extended the warmest hospitality to the Prior, despite the fact that few of them had much sympathy for or knowledge of Christianity. Though suffering from a severely swollen knee, the Prior spent a day doing zazen at Ryutaku-ji, the temple of Soen Nakagawa Roshi, whose disciple Eido Tai Shimano has founded a large and beautiful Zen center in New York City, as well as a retreat in the Catskills.

In 1971 the Prior's book of conversations was followed by *The End of Religion,** a volume in which a mature and theocentric Catholicism is proposed. In this book, remarkable for a number of reasons, not the least of which is the attached *permissu superiorum ordinis,* the fruit of the Prior's Oriental pilgrimage has fully ripened.

He concludes his autobiographical explorations: "If I were asked for the impossible, to sum up what I mean by ultimate religion in a phrase, I would say that it consisted in *enlightened openness.* But what, it may be asked, of love, which Jesus himself exemplified and insisted on so often? The answer is that love is not so much a challenge or a goal, something we can achieve and practice, helped by divine grace; it is a profound psychological problem. The love that Jesus advocated was *selfless.* And that brings us into a different world—precisely that of rebirth, authenticity, realization, enlightenment, salvation, whichever term we prefer. It is significant that in the prayer that Jesus taught his

* Dom Aelred Graham, *The End of Religion* (New York, Harcourt Brace Jovanovich, 1971).

disciples the word 'love' does not occur. The stress is on openness to God—'Thy kingdom come, Thy will be done'—and similarly with man, the removal of all barriers—'Forgive us our debts as we forgive . . .' Unselfless love, the best that most of us have to offer most of the time, is always flawed, however imperceptibly, by self-interest; it easily falls away into some form of paternalism or mere 'do-goodism.' . . . The Buddhist 'compassion,' it seems to me, has richer implications than all but the supreme form of Christian love. Christianity at the level of practice only rarely overcomes its theoretical dualism between man and God, between man and man. Here we may note in passing that 'sin,' a very Christian concept, has the same derivation as 'sunder,' and means *separation.* Sin is what separates us from God and from man, and it may well be, as the ecologists are insistently pointing out, from nature itself. . . .

"Openness is all—openness to the play of existence, whether it is manifested as God, as man, as animals or the world of nature; not openness as mere passivity but as the response of enlightened understanding, which will often lead to vigorous and sustained activity. Such openness enables us to realize that individual self-hood—the ego closed in on itself—is illusory. Only in piercing through this illusion, which is a function belonging not to the will but to the mind, can I become a loving person—as distinct from a man of good will, whose genuine affections are restricted to a comparatively small circle of relatives, friends, and acquaintances. . . .

"By . . . enlarging and purifying our consciousness, we learn to see life from the standpoint of total existence and accordingly to know the truth that makes us free."*

Buddhists are not truncated, unconscious Christians, as some modern Christian theologians suggest. On the other hand, I do not agree with Buddhists who believe that all Christians are simply

*Graham, *The End of Religion,* pp. 261–64.

second-rate Buddhists, too dogma-ridden to be capable of true enlightenment.

"What is the function of a Zen master?" people interested in Zen inquire. A Chinese monk on meeting a well-known master for the first time was asked where he came from. The monk replied that he was from the place where the Sixth Patriarch had been teaching. Then the master inquired, "What have you brought with you?" The monk answered, "That which was never lost even before I went." The master further inquired, "Then why did you find it necessary to go at all?" The monk replied, "If I had not gone to the place where the Sixth Patriarch was teaching, how would it have been possible for me to realize that it had never been lost?" At some point in our lives, contact with a person wise and experienced in the ways of the spirit may well be essential. Must our teachers share our ritual and dogmatic preferences? What about a Zen Catholic roshi for a Buddhist or, conversely, a Zen Buddhist roshi for a Christian?

The Christian or Buddhist roshi who can teach without teaching, and who returns from his search in the dragon's cave with empty hands, is the teacher with integrity and enlightenment. He will know how to leave the business of conversion, of "making" Christians and "teaching" the Buddha's enlightenment, to the real Teacher and true Roshi—the Holy Spirit, the Buddha nature.

POSTSCRIPT

As Dogen Zenji, the founder of Eihei-ji temple, watched a lighted incense stick slowly dissolve into ashes while he knelt beside the body of his dead mother, the evanescence of existence pressed a koan on him with compelling urgency: "Who am I?" In the course of a lifetime, each person faces one great basic koan about the meaning of life in general and of his own life in particular, an existential question involving just this present moment in time and space. It can be said that there are many different kinds of important koans in life; but it is just as true to say that there is one koan only, the multiplicity being an illusion. Unquestionably, the koans that most deeply affect us are our own. Nevertheless, no koan is unique, and those who face an important koan with courage and perseverance inevitably share some measure of their pain and their realization with others.

In this book I have introduced many koans, at least one of my own and some of other people's. The author's childhood descent into the blue dragon's cave was precipitated by the sight of a bewildered, screaming pig with blood pouring from one eye. An elderly Russian faces the rejection of his last and most intimate gift to his dead wife. A distinguished Bostonian in his lifelong quest for strength and virtue observes that "it is not possible to make a rope of sea sand or to make a wet towel stand on end no matter how long one tries." After many years of monastic endeavor, a Benedictine monk is persuaded that "if we consciously watch ourselves, strive directly to eliminate egocentric thoughts, the trouble increases, as it would by contemplating one's own unattractiveness in a mirror. . . . Even prayer and devotion, though they can bring us nearer to the root of the matter, have not the power to provide a final solution." Then there is that wise and charming relative of George Bernard Shaw who encounters another sort of koan during a confrontation with a Japanese Zen roshi and his sakè bottle. Another kind of koan found in these pages is the queries of a Christian-turned-Buddhist-turned-Christian as she contemplates the death mask of her late Buddhist teacher.

The Dharma eternally speaks to different people in as many different ways, through their own koans as well as through the koans of others. The pursuit of enlightenment is a way without end, a way that embraces the beings and things all around us, which we must come to see through a Buddha's eyes, our own enlightened eyes. "Truly to understand the self," wrote Dogen Zenji, "is to forget the self; to forget the self is to be enlightened by all things."

Our own Buddha nature draws us toward an ever greater realization of the horizons and possibilities of the eternal life of Great Naturalness. "If the Bodhisattva cannot attain Nirvana until even the grass itself has become enlightened," runs a Tibetan koan, "will he ever be free?" When we find ourselves in the depths of the dragon's cave, fearful and alone, it is easy to forget that

"Though we cannot see the Way, it is ever before us:
enlightenment is neither near nor far
and this is all we need to know."

(Sekito, *Sandokai*)

ACKNOWLEDGMENTS

For permission to reprint excerpts from Zen Catholicism *and* The End of Religion *by Dom Aelred Graham I am grateful to the author and to the publisher, Harcourt Brace Jovanovich, New York. I am also grateful to Dom Aelred Graham for permission to quote from his correspondence. I wish to thank Akiko Murakata for bringing to my attention the letters of William Sturgis Bigelow, as well as other materials pertaining to him. The excerpts from two nineteenth-century diaries in chapter three were made accessible through the efforts of the late Eunice J. Cabot, who edited the unpublished journals of my great-grandmother Mary Josephine Faxon and my grandmother Josephine Forbush.*

The "weathermark" identifies this book as having been planned, designed, and produced at the Tokyo offices of John Weatherhill, Inc., 7-6-13 Roppongi, Minato-ku, Tokyo 106. Book design and typography by Dana Levy. Composition by the Samhwa Printing Co., Seoul. Printed by the Kenkyusha Printing Co., Tokyo. Bound at the Makoto Binderies, Tokyo. The text is set in 11-point Monotype Baskerville, with Baskerville and hand-set Optima for display.